immaculate
immortality

Channeled Dark Feminine Poetry

Lennan Smith

Disclaimer

This book is intended for entertainment purposes only. The information, suggestive text or ideas expressed in this book are not intended to be substituted for professional care. This book does not offer medical, psychological or emotional advice. The author accepts no liability or responsibility for any outcomes, consequences or mode of action taken from the use of context provided in this book.

Written and Illustrated by Lennan Smith
©2024

Contents

Dedicated to Her.

May Chaos Guide Me Through The Void.

And Hecate Light My Way.

Tiamat Take Me To New Depths,

And Nyx To Far Away.

Ereshkigal Holds The Keys To My Death,

While Persephone Brings My Spring.

Help Me To Say My Piece, Lilith,

On The Backs Of Cailleach's Winter Wings.

Baba Yaga Send Me Home With Boons,

Standing With Medusa's Might.

May Medea Teach Vengeance Swift,

While The Moirae Hold My Strings Tight.

Goddesses & more

The dark feminine is a mystery. Working with Her and allowing Her into our spiritual lives unveils this mystery. Exploring the paths of the dark feminine provides meaningful resilience. She is timeless and formless yet embracing and purging. Her omnipresence fills the vessel that is us while also being the vessel. Whether She is silent, screaming, or smiling after us, we see Her for all the archetypes She is and can be in our lives. We discover, replenish, nurture, and dream with Her. We yearn for Her through the many guises she possesses. We seek to understand Her wisdoms. She occupies many vocations in spiritual practice, such as that of the healer, shapeshifter, mother, queen, priestess, sorceress, and more. She creates and destroys. She saves. She is paradox.

She is enigma. She walks alongside us, never to be locked in, or placed in a corner. She is the soul. The dark feminine within is sung forth, written down, and prayed to in all forms of reverential devotion.

The dark feminine embodies potent energies that resonate throughout the universe. As a palpable presence, She crackles at the seams of reality, eagerly anticipating sacred infusion. She is insatiable in body, mind, and spirit, seeking sustenance for all. Her energetic dominion permeates through the senses, and She delights in mystical potions of energetic allowances. She resides in the energetic vortex of the crossroads, where the winds of fate converge, and amidst the brilliance of celestial bodies, down to the entropic principles at the very core of galaxies. The dark feminine represents the embodiment of energetic omnipotence, a force that spans across dimensions and infuses every corner of existence with Her potent presence.

She is a spirit that transcends boundaries. Whether She represents a specific or unspecified being or deity, She encompasses all realms, serving as a sovereign and guardian here and in other times and spaces. She holds the basis in matters of the heart and soul, and it is here where she longs to reside. The power of the being lies in knowing and belief. When inviting her to perform under the developing soul, She thrives. We commune, pray, thank, and seek with the spiritual, finding solace and strength in Her presence. Bask in the light offered by Her grace, allowing it to illuminate the path ahead. Revel in Her darkness to embrace the chthonic.

The feminine is a powerful entity with profound mental capabilities. She encourages us to release any shame or guilt associated with our actions and decisions, guiding us through the darkness toward understanding and acceptance. She permeates our consciousness and delves into the depths of the collective and personal unconscious, embracing the shadows and urging us to explore alongside Her. The aim of the psychological feminine is to unlock and embrace our true selves, offering us mental clarity and insight. In times of psychological warfare and war care, She stands as a symbol of strength and guidance, providing support and understanding amid turmoil.

Working with deities, beings, and spirits can be a deeply moving and empowering experience. They serve as profound reminders of the paths we have chosen, the destinies we have been given, or the hardships we have endured. These powerful entities exist on the periphery of our awareness, yet their presence is always felt within the depths of our souls. Their beauty lies in their remarkable ability to collaborate with us mortals, crafting new realities that intertwine with our own. The dark feminine, with her many multifaceted faces, embodies a captivating and enigmatic presence that transcends the ordinary.

Author's Note
There are many names with spiritual or cultural significance that we could use. The ones I have included here are important in my spiritual and magical practice. They include goddesses, beings, and archetypes. Channeled messages, poems, prayers, and devotional letters have come through each one, giving me insight into their essence.

These reflections have transformed since reveling in them. Sometimes the titles turn to epithets for chanting and praying. Other times, they have inspired other creative works. Each page renders itself vocally, emotionally, spiritually, psychologically, and hauntingly perceptive. She works through me. I become a conduit for Her. As I explore my life and the wonderment therein, She becomes a participant and observer.

I hope you utilize the note pages after each subsequent being, should you so choose, to form new names, prayers, chants, songs, word plays, and anything else your heart desires.

I have included energetic temples for the main chapters. These act as sacred spaces. I use these temples to connect to domain and crawl, swim, hunt, or lurk in order to find and connect with Her on Her turf. May they provide guidance as you trek to their beautiful realms.

Within this space, you will not encounter traditional stories, myths, or legends. Engaging with deities, beings, or spirits requires a deep understanding and personal gnosis. The interpretation of these narratives forms an integral part of the spiritual journey. The channeled messages possess an enchanting and uplifting quality.

It is essential to closely contemplate the multifaceted archetypes contained within. These penetrating words convey respect, unwavering dedication, and encompassing guidance. She communicates with us and through us, offering an opportunity to connect with her various attributes and to invoke Her presence.

Chaos

Virgin Chaos

Break The Hearts
On Marrow Sting.
Petals Dance
On Outward Spring.
Coils Of Sky
Seize Firmament's Wing.
Anchor Doth Well
In Sharpness Fling.
Chaos Tether
Vibratory Slings.
Trumpets Sound
As Virgins Sing.
Across The Cosmos
Quivering Rings.
Pulse Led Stares
Blood Clings.
Truth Devout
Occurrences Will Bring.

Universal Crossing.

Our Lady of the Abyss

O Hail,
Our Lady of the Abyss.
Deep and Dark.
Conjuring from Base's Roil.
Toil for Those Lost
In Time and Place.
Perpetual Waves
Seed the Sands
In Assurance.
Remoteness Casts
Lines Out to Ether's Low.
Draft Expanses
Reverence Profound.
Spit up Foam
Of Cosmoses
Unfathomable.

Queen of Void

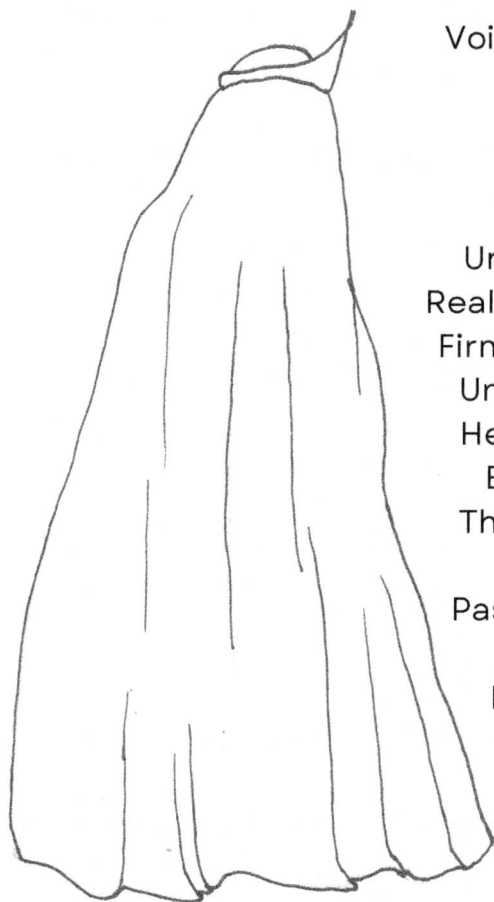

Slip Back Your Bow
String
On The Brink Of
Sanity's
Cusp.
Voided Melodies
Grasp
At Strings
Of Chaos.
Tight With
Unmanifested
Realities Yet To Be.
Firm Your Target,
Unmatched By
Heaven's Dale.
Breaths Let
The Arrows Of
Growth
Pass The Canal
Of
Expansion.
Onward.

Mother Ether

Mother Ether
Let Your Children
Wander Aimless
Across The Milky Clouds.
Turn Towards Their
Potentiality.
Upturn Your Hands
For Unconditional Embrace.
O Intense, O Unmeasured, O Macrobian.
Mother Ether
Full of Exuberant Profundity.
Cast Your Spell
Upon The Untold Hours.
Aid Those In Eternal
Motions Fair.
Timeless Mother Ether
Let Your Children
Experience Your Unfailing
Infinities.
In The Name Of
Immutable Bounds.
Sit Ita Summus.

Enchantress of Formless Darkness

Cloaked in Darkness.
Cloaked in Might.
Swirls The Entrails
Of Dusts Divine.
Enchant The Deep
Void of Formless Skies.
Magic Orbs In Hands
Abound.
Cast The Spell
Make Darkness Fly.
Bring Forth Airs
From Vessel Bloat.
Mesmerize The Guarded
Blackness Shrouds.
Thrill Touched
On Alluring Centers.
Horizons Chatter
Obscurity Writ.

Veiled Enigma

Veiled Enigma
I Hear You In My Blood.
Greater Than Before
Times Unimaginable.
Mystery Hovers
Over Voided Wilderness.
Orbit the Souls
Of Those Hindered
By Conundrum's Dalliance.
Amplitude Rampant
With Capacity Unknown.
Spaces Fill Extended
Versions Of Swept Widths.
Tease the Senses
On Staple Ruts.
Question the Calls
Quandary Unexplained.
Evermore.

Mother of Dark Mists

In The Scope Of Your Vast Embraces
I See The Trails Of Dust
Flying Ever Forward From
Bosoms Fraught On Endangered Roads.

Wielding Peace In Mindless
Scares Of Darkness Specking
Chatter From Glorified Lips.

In The Scales Of Timeless Brumes
I Hear Speak
Things I Cannot Name
Rendering Eerie Ambience.

Tattling Chides Of Your Tongues
I Taste Your Neutrality
Spitting Mist Sermons.

In Your Harsh Landscapes
I Feel The Abrasive Fog
Forming on Dark Energy
Culminating Scopes Of Essentiality.

Gale Goddess

Gale Force Goddess
Drenched In Universe's Grasp.
Hold Breaths Aloft
Silent as My Gasps.

Blow Across My Cheek
All Your Designs.
Pick Up Speed
The Gusts Are Intertwined.

Goddess of the Gale
Raise the Penultimate Zephyr.
Rush The Current
Drafts Unyielding Weather.

May The Breeze Remember
What Unrevealing Squall.
Dance of the Winds
Holding Universes In Thrall.

Conjurer of Pregnant Shadows

Deep In Shadows
Cloy and True.
Your Heart Renders
A Silent Clue.
Deep in Wombs
Growing and Through.
Birth the Galaxies
Inside of You.
(x3)

Prima Materia Matron

Matron of First Matter
Anatomized the Futures Coming.
Ubiquitous Chaos.
Study the Four Elements
Of Confused Masses
Dense in your Longing.
Collect Tears of the Righteous
Questing in Heaven's Bosom.
Acid Rain Falls
In the Mouth
Of your Lovingly Maw.
Strange Vapors Escalate
Guiding the Formless
To Ether's Bower.

Madam of Undivided Mass

Original Madam

Of Undivided Mass.

You Unfathomable Immortal

Drenched in Chaotic Pasts.

Cast Be to You.

O, Matter and Energy.

Watcher Of the Worlds

Confirming Our Memories.

Lady of Chasms.

Progenitor of Life.

Quantify the Realms

With Cosmologies Rife.

Quintessence Queen

Billions of Years,
But What is Time?
Hand Over Mouth,
Screaming with Sublime.

Home in the Nothing,
Skies Void of Traps.
Caught in the Cosmos
Between the Gaps.

Circling Immortal Drains,
Our Quintessence Queen.
Shields of Energy
From Those Who Intervene.

Cast Your Shadows
Bring The Valor.
Guide All Forms.
For All Matter.

Weaver of Ageless Entropy

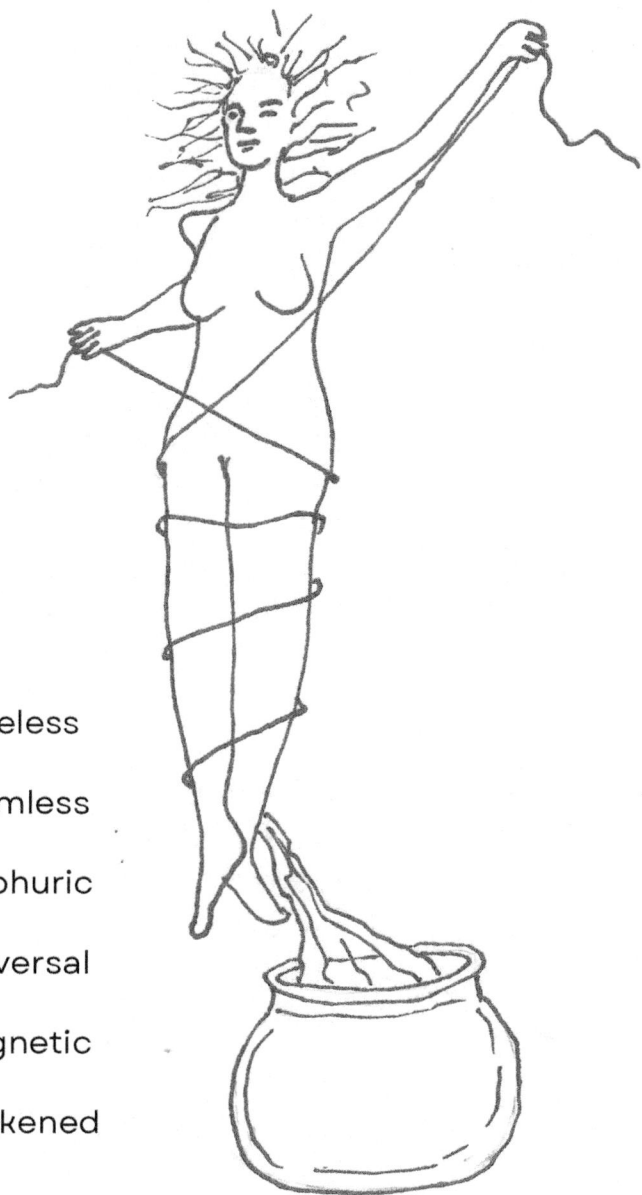

Ageless

Formless

Sulphuric

Universal

Magnetic

Awakened

She of Shapeless Heaps

Distorted Shade
Of Shapeless Heaps
Twisted Darkness
Of Boundless Leaps

She Calls Forth the Void
And Cuts Past the Fog
Her Hair is Covered in Darkness
Soft Laughs From Universe's Prologue.
Motion Ceaseless in Her Embrace
The Swirls Defines the Warps.
Her Gaze Sways Upward
Along Vale's Records.

Distorted Shade
Of Mangled Weeps
Contorted Darkness
Of Immeasurable Sleep

Wet-nurse of Rarefied Winds

Windless Might
Utters Across
the Voided
Chasms.
Do Your Worst.
For the Void
Calls
Forth It's Own.
Squeeze the
Teet of
Vanquished
Winds.
Rarefied in Its
Afterbirth.
Nurture the
Offspring
Of Universes.

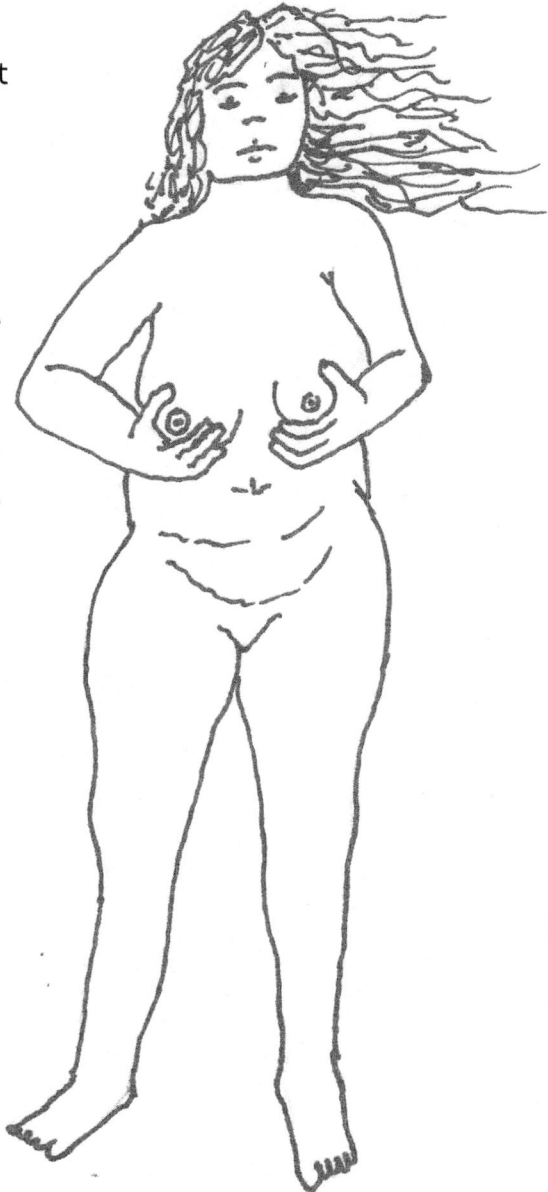

Empress of Emptiness

Listless Mass Of Cloudless Skies
The View From your Throne.
Gone is The Search for Light
In The Blank Canvases
Of Galaxies Forgotten.

Lethargic Reign Of Unjeweled Crowns
The Veil Of The Unknown.
Gone is The Quests For Entropy
In The Languid Existences
Of Dark Cosmos.

Catatonic Emptiness Of Vastness
The Droning Tones.
Gone is The Journey For Materiality
In The Voided Spaces
Of Nature's Zones.

Vacuums Of Deserted Horizons
The Suction Of Loneliness.
Gone is The Pursuit For Cures
In The Stark Capacities
Of Distant Comets Shone.

Awaken at the genesis of creation. You are flying, hovering above a black hole. Eerie, sonic, white noise is all you can hear, for your senses have become obsolete. You are safe from the entropy. However, you can feel the pull of gravity trying desperately to suck you in. Radiation bounces around you and the surrounding space. You call out a name in this void space but it becomes silent screaming.

You are exhausted from the constant tug of creations bliss and want to close your eyes. You can not. All You can do is hover.

She is here, in this empty space between sleep and awake, a presence just inside the event horizon.

TEMPLE OF TEMPORAL INFINITY

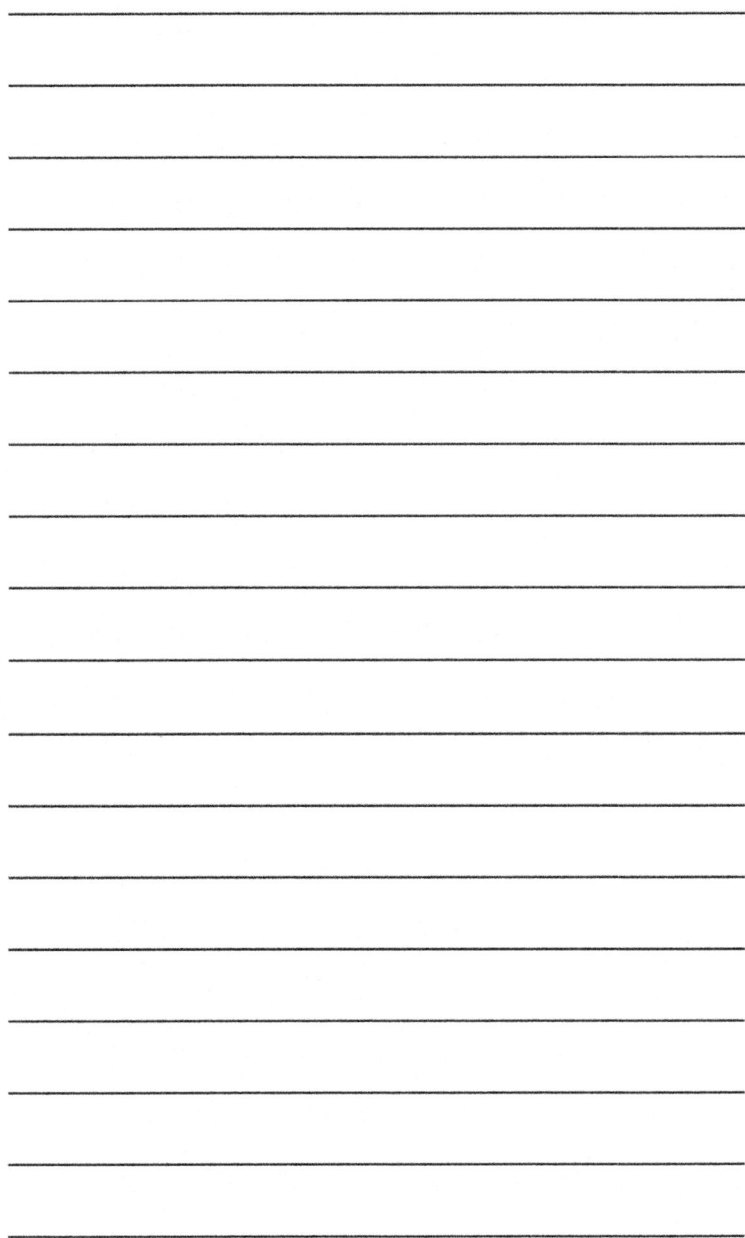

Tiamat

Our Lady of the Salty Sea

Cruel Mistress Of The Salty Seas,
Submerge Unto Us A Temporal Existence.

Entities Wrought Of Your Salinity,
Peace Be To Us In Your Vastness.

Hoist The Stage Of Life's Mortality,
Continuous Moments Cast Pallidness.

Flaccid Waves Conjure Needed Stillness,
Dead Calm Spans The Hourglass.

Set The Moon At High Tides,
Laughing In Crescent Slumbers.

Swimming Underway To Render Solaces,
Shift Your Hospitable Shape.

Stretch Your Waters Across All Lands,
For They All Lead To You.

Serpentine Source

Immense, Your Pivotal Role,
Crossing The Oceans Of The Worlds
Cleansing What Needs You.

You, The Source Of All,
Expanding The Waters Of Time
Exiled To Depths Unknown.

You, The Apex Of Creations,
Building The Wise Straits Of Materials
Processing What Is Birthed.

Colossal Serpent Whirling
Brackish Current Of Dominions
Docking At Love's Shores.

Draconian Sea Witch

Sea Witch! Sea Witch!
Call Me Down To Your Depths,
(x3)

Queen of Scales

Galaxies From Dragon Tails
Queen Of Scales.

Following Your Iridescent Sails
Queen Of Scales.

Avoiding Your Obnoxious Rales
Queen Of Scales.

You Who Always Prevails
Queen Of Scales.

From All Comparisons Rale
Queen Of Scales.

Beast Surrendering Details
Queen Of Scales.

You, Who Never Fails
Queen Of Scales.

Goddess of the Deep

Collecting Driftwood In Your Name

Collecting Seashells In Your Name

Collecting Fossils In Your Name

Collecting Seaweed In Your Name

Collecting Fish Bones In Your Name

Collecting Salt In Your Name

Collecting Sea Glass In Your Name

Collecting Shark Teeth In Your Name

Collecting The Gulfs In Your Name

For The Goddess Of The Deep

Begetteress

Begettress Of Monstrous Scions,
You Who Would Destroy And Birth All Life
In Your Primordial Seas.

Wade Along Coastlines Across All Worlds.

Mate With Creations' Sweet Fresh Waters
And Bring Forth All.

Begettress Of Heinous Souls,
You Who Would Destroy And Birth All Life
In Your Pristine Oceans.

Trek Along Estuaries Across All Worlds.

Mate With Creations' Sweet Fresh Waters
And Bring Forth All.

Wielder of Oceans

Wielder Of Oceans,
Set Us All Free.
Drown Us In Your Tears,
Cast Us To All Seas.
Spring Forth The Atoms,
Growing In The Tides.
Wielder Of Oceans,
Please Be Our Guide.
(x3)

She Who Bears All

Birthed In Your Crevasse,
In The Wide Great Blue,
I Stand Alone There,
Enjoying The View.

Life Begins Rolled,
In Wonderment Pursues,
My Breaths Be Cast,
The Winds You Blew.

For When I Die,
I'll Get What I'm Due,
Like All Waters,
I'll Return To You.

Our Mother of Shining Waters

Shimmering Memory Of Waters Deep,

Sovereign Of The Dark Sweeps.

Ancient Soul Of Shining Waters,

Come To Us Your Forever Daughters.

Sail Be To The Mighty Oracle,

Glimmer Bright And Durable.

Our Mother Matriarchal,

Loving In Your Sparkle.

Beaming At Horizons Found,

Within All Oceans Abound.

Lamia of Sodden Skins

Slip The Tongues

On Sodden Skins.

Birth Cosmic Oceans

Upon Your Breadth.

Soaking.

Guarding The Hearty Vials

Of Tasty Volatile Lots.

Whet Our Appetites With

Flourishing Expediency.

Drowning.

Thanks Be To You, Lamia.

Designer of Worlds

Designing The Worlds
From Your Bowels.
Conjure The Waters,
Of Your Vast Prowls.

(x3)

Autotelic Authority

From All That Has Come
Thanks Be To You.
Your Saline Wisdom
Rings Ever True.

In Rivers Converging
Bring Your Salty Gulfs.
Take Notions Aboard
You Who Demand Results.

In Your Vast Midst
You Swirl The Recesses.
Roiling The Deep
Trenches Ever Possesses.

Channeled Gulch Creatrix
Down In The Trench.
With Ocean Tides
Slap And Wrench.

Sorceress of the Wild Expanse

Rippling Under The Full Moon,

I Petition You.

Hear My Undulating Call,

I Ask You.

Waving My Teether Waves

I Beseech You.

Standing In Your Ebb,

I Solicit You.

Thrashing About Your Cruelty,

I Plead You.

Floating About Your Ethereality,

I Pray To You.

Baroness of Brine

Weave Slick Brine.

Emerge From Primal Natures Bore.

Ancient Fates Last For Times

Down In The Crypts Of All Oceans.

Wander The Petty Bioluminescent.

Guard The Reefs Of Ageless Yielding

For Future Seasons Of Depths.

Protect Seaweed Crowns

Circling Your Worldly Heads.

Nests Cast In Epochs

Catching Prey To Sustain Peace.

Witch of the Waves

Cast Your Oscillating Spell
Upon Us, Ever Your Brethren.

Span Oceans Of Time
Upon Us In Our Mortal Bodies.

Ripple Surging Your Bewitchment
Upon Us, Ever Our Liege.

Trancing Our Allegiances
Upon Us, Swell Your Enchantments.

Charming Coifing Tidals
Upon Us In Our Mortal Bodies.

Whirl Your Sorcery Surfs
Upon Us, Ever Our Witch
Of The Waves.

TEMPLE OF PRIMORDIAL WATERS

Awaken on the shores of creation. You are lying on hot sand. Hot, balmy waters ebb and flow on your feet. Nothing but void and galaxies in the skies overhead. The line of the horizon is the only earthly thing you see. You sit up on your knees and send out a soft prayer to Tiamat. You cup your hands in the water and it shimmers with magic. You stare reverently down into the them. Lost in your watery reverie, you hear a splash nearby. You raise your gaze and notice the semblance of a tail descend into the depths. She's here, just under the surface. You feel her here at the edge of it all, where it all began.

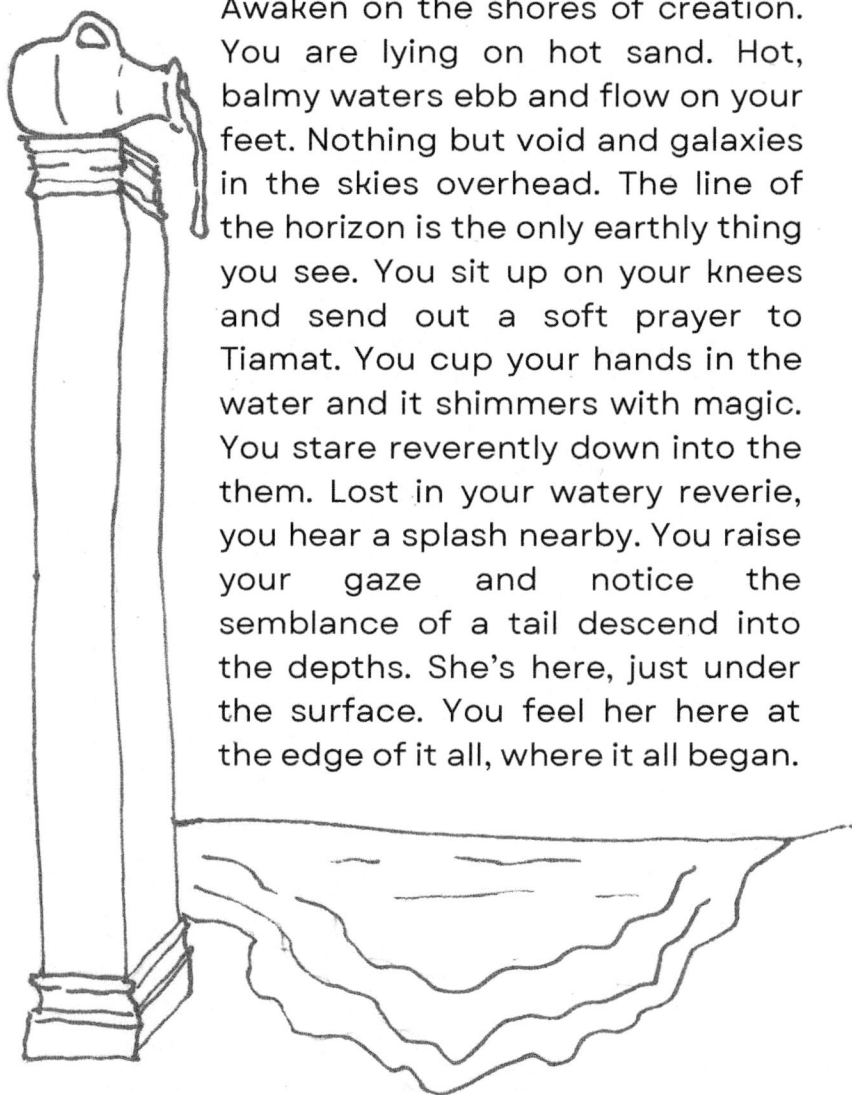

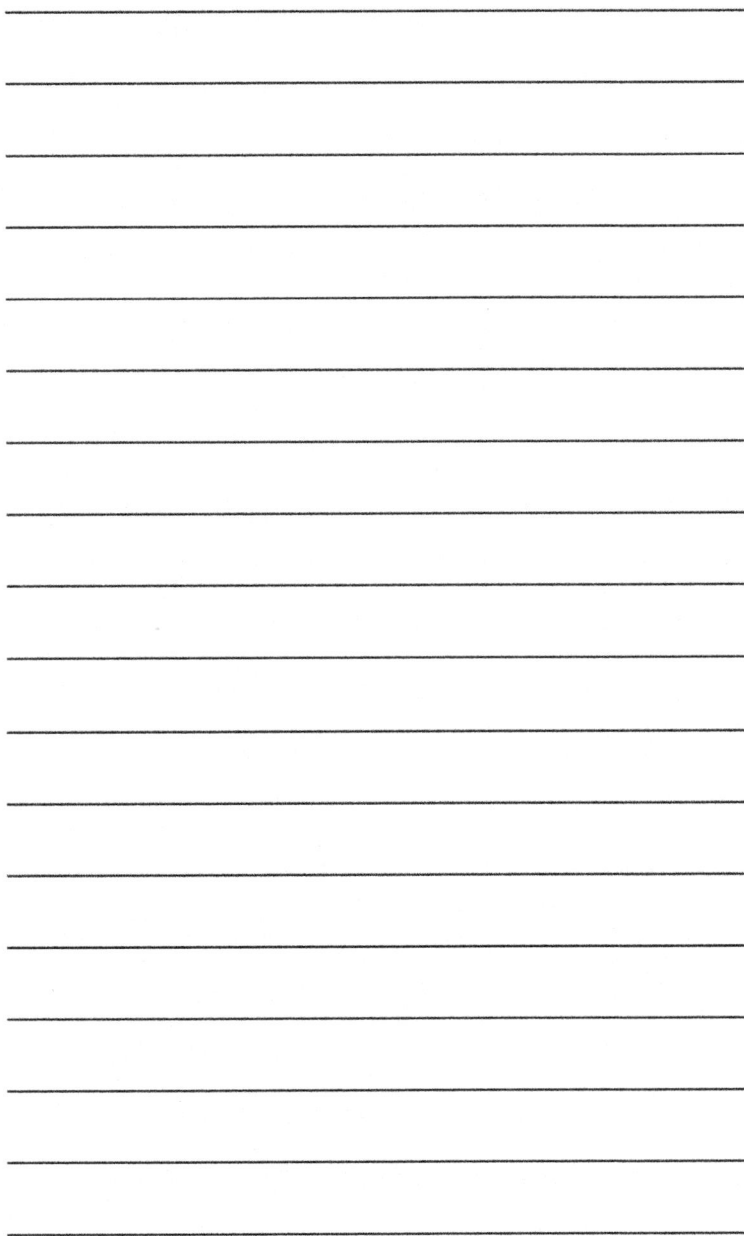

Nyx

Our Lady of Heaven's Vault

Crumbling Ceiling Of Heaven's Vault
Laying Open Upon My Face.
Stars In My Other Eyes,
Tears Streak Like Comets
Across My Inky Cheeks,
Linger Here.

Night Waits For No One.
As Pink Skies Turn Purple,
Rushing To Midnight,
With A Savior's Yawn,
Wide In The Throat,
Hunger Here.

Where Ethereal Atoms Dwell.
While Nocturnal Creatures
Dance The Passion Of Darkness.
The Elements Know,
My Inner Heart's Toil,
Wish Here.

Star Virgin

Stars Are Rescued
Stars Are Fixed
Dying Slowly
Needs No Tricks

Virgin Rides
Across The Night
Darkness In Hand
Races Her Flight

She Holds No Fear
This Inevitable Soul
With Swift Ascent
Her Domain Is Whole

All The Night
Her Breadth Did Last
Down She'll Go
When Dawn Is Cast

Mother of Obscurity

Force Yourself Into The Secrets of the Night.

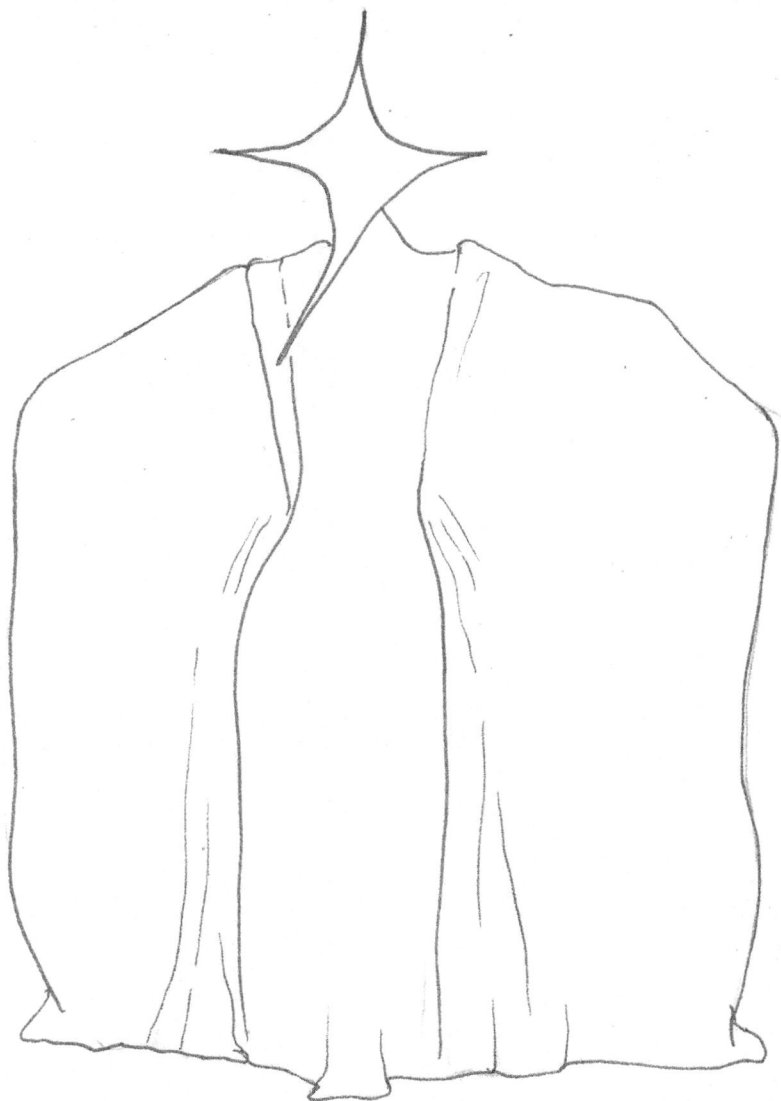

Lady of Winged Night

Unfurl The Winged Night
Sweeping Forward In Day's Last Rays
Flying Hither Toward Horizons
Gather The Mists Of Heavens
Subdue The Laws Of Earth And Sky
Meet In The Middles

Rip Apart The Clouds
Tap Dance The Stars Into Existence
Staring At Radiation's Spring
Awe—
In Reverent Soars' Chariot

Take Back Sleep's Fever Dream
Cloaked In The Veil Of Twilights
Course Laid Conceived Unions
In Great Cosmic Eggs
Waiting On You To Be Ever-Born

Queen of Galaxies

Queen Of Galaxies, On This Night
Take Me To Your Greatest Heights.

Send Me Forth Into Your Arms,
Conjuring In Forming Stars.

My Breath Be True,
I Stand In Your Glorious Views.

I Offer You My Presence Here,
Arms Unfolded With No Fear.

And Even With No Light,
Your Love Is Ever Bright.

Show Me My Fate,
Under Your Dark Weight.

Painter of Twilights

Paint Twilight Frescos
With Scepters Of Your Sovereignty.
Depend On The Inevitability
Of Night's Bejeweled Pigments.

Colors Coalesce In Your Warm Embrace
With Stippled Stars Overhead.
Scour Souls Lost To The Night
Fables Told In Discarded Divinities.

Never Was A More Beautiful
Canvas Protracted Over All Faces.

Piratess of the Starry Skies

Plunder The Skies
Buried In Depths
Cannon Fire Bursting of Stars
Cruising Sky Compass

Spoils Of Havens Wrought
Pillage Stardust
Swashbuckling Otherworldly Planets
All Galaxies Tell Tales

Conjurer of Nebulosity

Night Renders True The Sonic Sounds
Subjugate Amorphous Gaseous Renown
Cosmos Must Birth Cosmos
And Designed Ends Of Time Is Wound

Conjure Down The Dark Spirits' Flight
Nebulous Growth Calling For Aching Night
Stars Must Yield Stars
And Brand A Dome Of Felt Sight

Arcane Blame In Day's Last Hours
Vague Haze In Resonant Screaming Power
Systems Manifest Systems
Behold Twilight's Greatest Tower

Prophetess of Pitch

Prophesize Pitch
Darkness Bewitch
Nightfall Witch
(x3)

Sorceress of Shade

Shadows and Shade
Hidden Yet Not Afraid
Take Me Away From The Day

Presence Be To You Now
Spell Cast Resounds
Bring Me To Your Brow

Lasting Be Your Might
Cyclical In Your Right
Deliver Me To Your Height

Screech And Howl
Cover Me In Your Cowl
Grant Me Your Foul

Through Stars And Ether
And As Night's Teacher
Usher Me Even Deeper

Midnight Witch

Withering Toward Midnight
Decaying Rotting Guile
Ask Again Dear Witch
Marching On In Love's Profile

Down To Rushing Stars
Bats Call Their Own
Flying Yonder There
In The Trees They Call Home

Light The Fire Wick
Embolden Goes The Flame
Nicking Ankles Dancing
Across The Merry Game

Invoke The Darkness
Draw Me Down To You
As I Descend, You Ascend
Becoming The Sweet Dew

Sunless Mystic

Mystic Of The Black Moon
Sophisticate Botanical Wrought
Sultry Flourishing Decay
Visional Night Shadows
Come to Me
Come To Me
Sunless Mystic

Masked In Garish Disorientations
Path Lay Barren At Me Feet
Behind The Dying Of Suns
Fortunes Yielding Growth
Come To Me
Come To Me
Sunless Mystic

Want Howls Haunting
Hunt Dark Towered Brethren
About Checked Nests
And Hidden Cosmic Eggs
Come To Me
Come To Me
Sunless Mystic

Sleepless Sighs Spellcaster

You Of Sleepless Sighs
Breaths Doth Rise
Across All Skies
Night's Spell Devise
(x3)

Our Lady of Immaculate Immortality

Or Lady Of Immaculate Immortality,
Possess Us In Your Bosom.
Our Eternal Lady Full Of Shadows,
Bless Us With Your Shining Darkness.
Queen Of The Night,
Oppress Us With Your Coming Mists.
Your Obscure Precision Hypnotizes
And Shakes Forth The Glowing Dance.
Seduce Us With Dreams.

Our Lady Of Immaculate Immortality,
Awaken Us To Your Bower.
Our Infinite Lady Full Of Shade,
Bless Us With Your Radiant Darkness.
Queen Of The Night,
Suppress Us With Your Coming Veil.
Your Somber Rigor Amazes
And Trembles Forth The Empty Void.
Tempt Us With Tomorrow's Hope.

Speaker of Night

Speak Forth The Night
Truths Sacrificed...

On The Eve Of The Equinox.
Serene Smoking Brume
Is Your Swallowing Breaths

Cover My Eyes With Your
Breeding Darkness...

Under The Black Ink Writ
Ravens Holds Power
Incanting Your Names

Brood Faithful The Night
Slain The Day...

Goddess of Never-Heard Sounds

Sounds Never Heard By Ears Not Listening
Goddess Speaks My Name
Punishing Claustrophobic Bliss—

In The Vapors Of My Mind
Limited In My Quantum Reverie
Sick With Night's Dark Sublime.

Render The Riddle Of Evenings
Coming Forth So Slowly
Watchful In Otherness Sensing—

Cast In The Moon's Shadow
Climbing Up To You
Reaching Black Canyons Narrow

Whispering Prevailing Nocturnal Skies
Where Its Always Caliginous
Dusk Conquering Cycles—

Infallible Unfathomability Rites
Reading The Signs Here
Creatured And Living Delights

Awaken in a lush bed. Moonlight is coming in from the window behind your bed. The spackled light of night is calling. You spin around and open the window. As you do, a rope ladder, leading high up into the sky, is pushed inside by an unseen force. You leave the comfort of the warm bed and grab the ladder. You pull yourself out of the window. There is nothingness below as if the room is suspended in midair. You hoist yourself out and hang precariously on the rope. For a long while you wait and hang. Finally, you begin the climb into the veil of night, closer and closer to her. She is here in the night among the stars.

TEMPLE OF STARSHINE

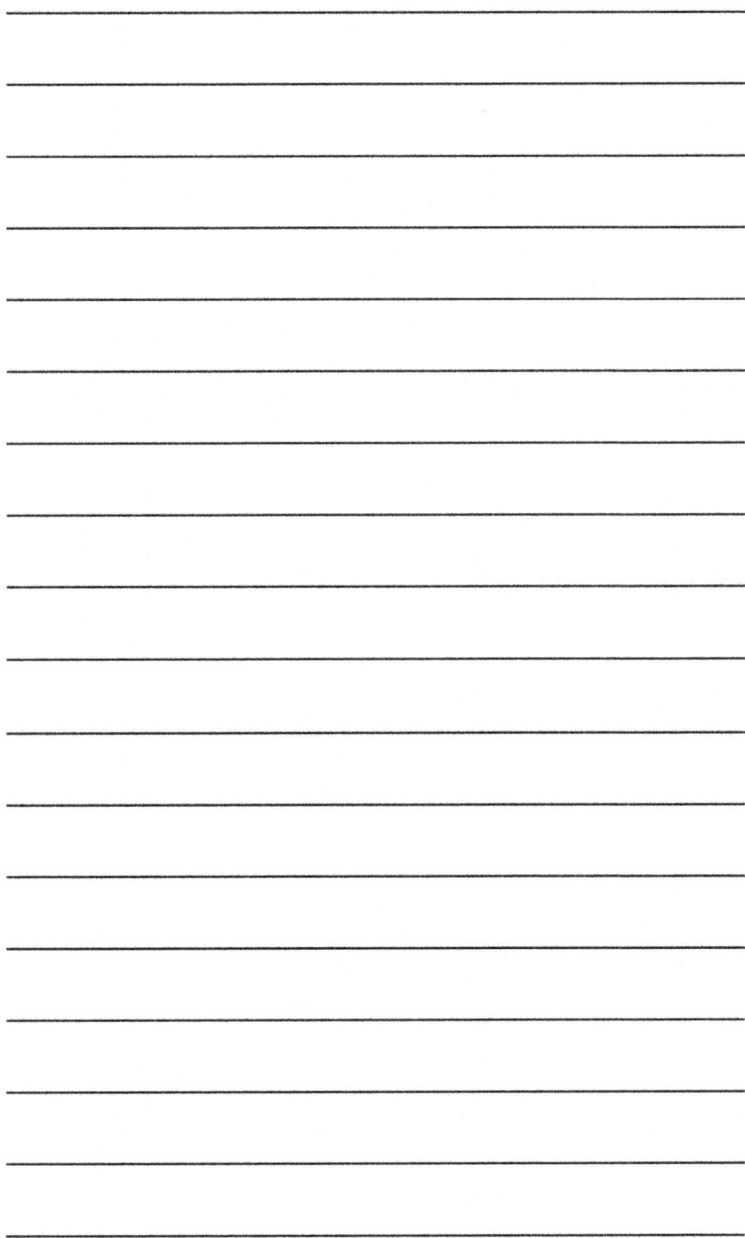

Hecate

Lady Of The Crossroads

Liminal Lady

Between Fire and Water.

Attach With Reverence

For the Liminal Spaces.

Walk in Power.

And Create the Paths

Combine Ever Opposed.

Trust The Process

Of The Threshold

You Who Knows The Boundaries.

As Above, So Below.

Desire the Expanding

Of The In-Between.

Dance Among The Verge.

Receive The Magic

Graced in The Locked Path.

Devote To Betwixt

The Fallen Breadcrumbs

That Lead To The Other Side.

Indomitable Queen of Witches

Interface With Us
Indomitable Queen of Witches.

Should We Take The Path
Should We Heed The Call
You Cover Us In Your Cloak
Embracing Us In Your Hall

Arise The Witches
Who Seek Your Grin
We Shall Find You
By Going Within

Interface With Us
Indomitable Queen of Witches

Weaver of the Wayside

Approach The Weaver.
See Her Stitches.
Intricacies From Settled Fingers.
Stable As The Warps.
Connecting As The Wefts.
The Weaver Knows
Her Bridge Building.

Approach The Weaver.
Present At The Wayside.
Tangled From Deft Hands.
Uniform As The Status Quo.
Linked By Magic.
The Weaver Knows
Her Crossings.

Approach The Weaver.
View Her Links.
Elaborate From Keen Mind.
Involved In Cunning Strings.
Affixed As Illusion.
The Weaver Knows
Her Boundaries.

Torchbearer

Kindred Be The Light.
That Shines From Torches.
Illuminating All Paths.
Evoking All Forces.
(x3)

She Who Holds the Keys

She Who Holds The Keys
Behind The Many Doors
Unlock New Awareness
Shaken To The Core

She Who Holds The Keys
Before Every Gate
Free The Ideas
Shutter To Await

She Who Holds The Keys
Around All Bends
Solve Inspirations
Seeing Each End

Guardian of the Dark Path

Persevere Trekking
Through Hard Times
Forward, Onward, Inward
The Remains Of The Left Behind

Endure Walking
Clutter May Stifle
Forward, Onward, Inward
The Catharsis Of The Trifle

Maintain Spine
Persist The Course
Forward, Onward, Inward
The Abyss Of The Source

Firm Be Footing
The Call You Did Hear
Forward, Onward, Inward
The Guardian Is Here

Protectress of Holy Death

Partnering With Death,
She Walks Along
The Merry Way Of Inevitability.
Flesh, Blood, and Bone
Are But Fleeting Occurrences.
Interpersonal, Impersonal
Death Be The All End.
Miasma Leavened
In Every Creature.
The Protectress Of Holy Death
Partners With The Edge
Deciphering Deficiencies
And Rapturous Demise.
She Holds Scarcities
Within Her Sheath.
Truth Be Granted in Oblivion
Beyond The Vision's Veil
Of The Holy Dead.

Mother of Magic

Mother, Mother!
Mother Of Magic.

Cast Your Spell
Upon The Many Faces
That Call For Enchantments.

Release Your Cant Statement.

Reveal Your Wonder.

Unveil The Illusions.

Of That Which is Unseen
Find Yours Where Logic Fails.
Discover Bewildered Kindred.

Mother, Mother!
Mother Of Magic.

Goddess of Convergence

Converge!

In Places Unknown
Reverences Atone
Through All Your Own
None Are Alone
Path Be Shown
Where Nothing Is Grown
Your Torches Shone
Ravens Flown
The Abyss Groan
Crossroad Throne
Marked By Stone
Seeds Are Sown
Buried Be The Bones
Singing All Tones
Final Flame Blown

Converge!

Lady of Lunar Requiem

Rites In Lunar Light
Restful As If In Dream
Command The Lucidity
Imagine Around The Periphery
Demand The Luminosity

Solemn Savioress

Solemn Savioress
Of The Grieving Heart

You Hear The Weeping
From In The Underworld

Lit From Within
You Traverse Darkened Paths

Collect The Broken
For The Sacred Rites

You The Oracle
With Visions True

Travel Dreams
Built on Bones

Rattle The Drums
Circling The Depths

Conjure The Forlorn
Evermore

Our Lady of Spiritual Depths

Deep Depths Drifter
Or Lady Of Spiritual Depths
Hecate, Hecate, Hecate

Tramp Trek Traveler
Our Lady Of Spiritual Abyss
Hecate, Hecate, Hecate

Ramble Rove Roamer
Our Lady Of Spiritual Caves
Hecate, Hecate, Hecate

Amble Aimless Anchor
Our Lady Of Spiritual Hollows
Hecate, Hecate, Hecate

Flit Float Flow
Our Lady Of Spiritual Chasms
Hecate, Hecate, Hecate

She Who Sees All Paths

Radiant Reflections
Be The Path Of All Truths
Scour The Unearthed
For Sights Divine
Into The Shadows

Follow You Down
Rocky Terrains

Radiant Reflections
Be The Paths Of All Schemes
Rummage The Grounds
For Painted Eternals
Into The Obscure

Follow You Down
Shaky Domains

Radiant Reflections
Be The Path Of All Gospels
Forage The Gardens
For Woven Infinities
Into The Mysteries

Three-formed Thaumaturge

Left, Right, Center
From Which You Enter
All The Ones
Who Will Surrender
To The Byways
In Each Phase

Attendant of the Underworld

Sepulchral Attendant

Awaiting The Traversing

Slow Slithering

Coated In Tartarus Gloom

Holding Hope In Souls

Kneeling In The Ways

Preparing For New Steps

Researching The Risks

Flames Be To Go

Hiding and Seeking

Initial Spaces Awaken

Guide The Encouraged

Following The Flow

Godmother of the Threshold

Godmother Rise

Guide Us Through Worlds
Summon Be The Model
Of Magical Roles
Participate In-Between Realms
Command Speak Sacred Vows
Make Meanings Broad
The Threshold Jaunt

Godmother Rise

Guide Us Through Cosmos
Assemble The Arts
Of Magical Duty
Engage Liminal Fields
Demand Speak Sacred Rites
Make Messages Obvious
The Verge Dance

Godmother Rise

Traversing Temptress

Tempting Be The Journey

Tempting Be The Way

Tempting Be The Paths

Tempting Be The Array

Tempting Be Shock

Tempting Be The Awe

Tempting Be The Foreseen

Tempting Be Prints Of Paw

Tempting Be The Marvel

Tempting Be A Spectacle

Tempting Be Traversing

Tempting Be The Delectable

Awaken in an empty darkened hallway. One foot in front of the other, torches light on either side of the stone walls. Goosebumps prick your skin as you trod.
You come to an open indoor, circular courtyard.
It is lit from a thousand torches in holders on high walls.
A labyrinth made of limestone marks lays before you.
Walk the maze.
You feel Her here, taking the steps with you. The heat from the torches soothes your chilled body. Stand in the center.

TEMPLE OF TORCHLIGHT REVERIE

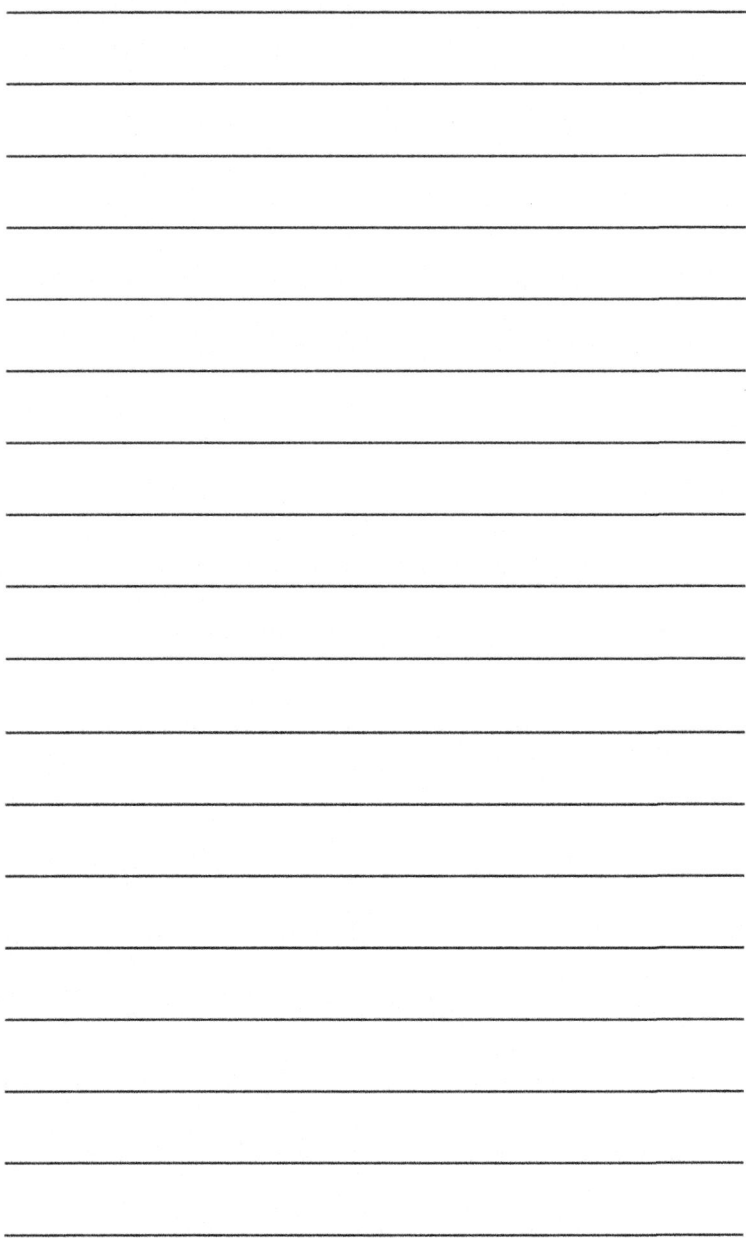

Ereshkigal

Our Lady of the Great Below

Our Lady Of The Great Below,
Commander Of Legions,
Standing Upon The Bastion Of Life,
Regard Me Your Unworthy Servant.

Our Lady Of The Great Beneath,
Commander Of Armies,
Standing Upon The Mouth Of Life,
Catch Me In Your Sharp Teeth.

Our Lady Of The Great Unseen,
Commander Of Hordes,
Standing Upon The Fortress Of Life,
Manage Me With Your Compassion.

Our Lady Of The Great Firmament,
Commander Of Throngs,
Standing Upon The Barrier Of Life,
Stain Me With Your Seal.

Countess Before The River

Wade Easily Along—
The River Of The Netherworld.
Floating Stings The Rapids Coursing
Down In Black Sea Swirls.

In The Bitterness—
Sounds Echo In Painful Destinies.
Vapid Conjuring, Lazy Streams
Down In Our Miseries.

Eyes Looking Back—
From The Distant Shores.
Life Passed By So Unsodden
Waving To Souls Poor.

Reaching The Destination—
Castle Of The Lonely Dead.
The Countess Waits On Lucid Docks
No More Tears Are Shed.

Mistress of Guarded Pandemonium

Where The Nectar
Of Mud Silt Pools
Cleanses Your
Palate.
Where The Dust
Falls Like Sugar
On Slowly Rotting
Tongues.
Where The Seeds
Of Red Fruit Lay
Forgotten.
Where The Souls
Of The Dead
Shall Never
Leave.
I, Mistress Here,
Will Guard
Pandemonium
Forevermore.

Caterer of Catacomb Mists

Mausoleum Stands Alone

Scattered Lay The Bones

Ancient As The Thrown Stones

Not So Much As A Tone

Guardians Of All The Unknown

The Dead All But Bemoan

Needless To Atone

Written In Sacred Tomes

Belonging To No One

No More Skills Are Honed

From Your Mist Throne

In The Eternal Catacombs

Queen of Foreboding

Foreshadowing Queen Of Foreboding
Forgotten Be The Cursed
You Who Knows Not Life
With Death You Are Well Versed

Never To Be Lead Astray
With Only One Quick Look
Embracing You In This Hour
I Am Written In Your Black Book

Hold Me Yonder Screaming
The Part That Won't Let Go
Sever All My Ties To Life
All Too Well You Know

For I Am Not A Humble Visitor
In This Realm You Call Your Own
Kiss Me On The Cheek
Then Let Me Wander Alone

Ruler of the Kur

Dragon Rider Aloft In Clouds Of Midnight
Contemplations Ride–
Down On The Backs Of Summoned Wings
Residing In Shoulder Blades Of Naught.
Cresting And Falling Above Fields Of Firelight
Cradling The Scales Of Hides Too Hot.
Kur Be The Place That Our Search Calls Us
Home Fluttering Time Standing Still.
Below The Great Furling Thing That Wants To
Annihilate The Tainted Inky Skies.
Down Deep In the Knowing Of Forever's Pain
Be Unto Death, Dear Dragon Rider.
Cast Spells On Smoking Nostrils Adrift In The
Vast Beneath Waiting For A Dark Opening.
Dismounting Shade's Acquiring Souls
Suckling At Forgotten Breaths To Take.
Sinking To Dark Ground Dominion's Rising
Sliver Of Moons Awaiting It's Queen.

Seeress of the Deceased

The Dead Be Not
Fools
You Will Abide By My
Rules.
Never To Be
Cruel.
(x3)

Conjurer of Compassion

Come To Me Sweet
Your Secrets Never To Be Told
I Rise To Your Pain
Whether You're Young or Old

I Take Your Earthly Burdens
And Shed You Of Your Layers
For Here You'll Remain
I Hear Your Every Prayer

Hasten To My Bosom
For I Am Cold In This Place
Ceaseless Love We Share
Come To Death With Grace

Governess of Souls

Look After Our Souls
Governess
Care For Our
Immortality,
Punish Us For Our
Sins.
For We Know Not Your
Realms And Rules.
Committed By
Humanities—
Teach Us The Ways
Of The Underworld
Take Us To The Lower
Places We've Never
Been.
Down To Where You
Kiss The Shadows
With Bare Feet.
Succumb Be The Last
Breaths Of Life That
Make You Continue
Here.
Feeding From Us, As We
Drink From You.

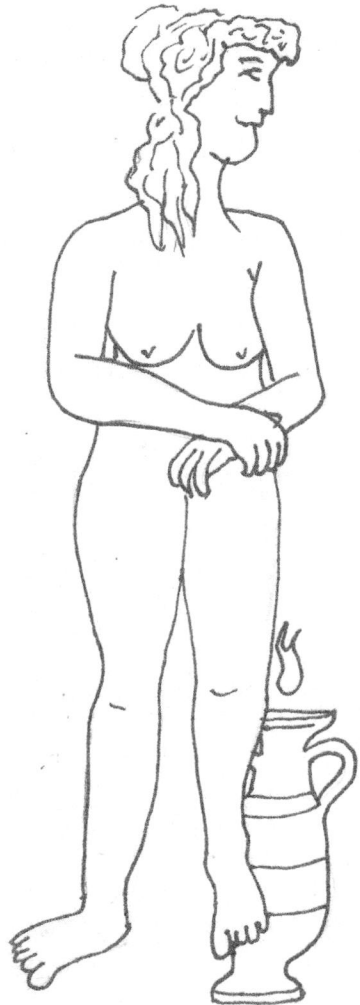

Watcher of the Chains

Ache The Death's Breath In The Chambers
Of The Heart, Red, No Longer Pumping.

Spasms Quake Rotting Corpses,
Voices Resting In Shares Of Darkness

Watch The Dead Hang There On Hooks
Slow To The Blinking Eyes

Quiet Holy Blessed Things, Skins On Chains
Watching The Dying Light

Mourn For The Sounds Of Decay Screaming
At The Mouths Of Nothing

Sire New Births In Span Of Three Days
Dream The Ever Wakeful

The Frozen Bouts Of Death Will Linger
Fancy On In Careful Preparation

Take From The Chains To Shelter
Love's Eternal Embrace Endlessness

Sybil of Solemnity

Guided By Hands Reading
The Apocrypha Of The Damned.
Allow The Incantations There
To Solemn Gazing Fortunes.
Speak At Last As If To You
The Spell Does Put To Rest.
Dire Needs Are The Deeds
Of The Dead Naming Truths.
Prophesize Omens Lurking
In Underworlds Absent Of Pleasure.
Nether Auger Of Earnest Blight
Waning Moons Cast No Shadow.
Look With All Eyes Searching
The Sickened Pale Stench.
Pass On Ceremony Conducting
Rituals Of The Holy Funeral Of All.

Goddess of The Seven Gates

Lose Your Spiritual Power,

Lose Your Earthly Power,

Lose Your Mental Power,

Lose Your Body Power,

Lose Your Love Power,

Lose Your Ego Power,

Lose Your Self Power,

All Who Wish Admittance

To The Goddess Of The Seven Gates,

Nude And Bowed.

Lady of Last Breaths

Have Mercy! On This Our Hour Of Death,

Lady Of Last Breaths.

Have Pity! At This The Crossroads Of Life,

Lady Of Last Breaths.

Have Sorrow! On This Eve Of Your Brevity.

TEMPLE OF CRYSTALLIZED DEATH

Awaken in the mouth of a dark cave. You can not see anything past your outstretched hand. You feel pulled to descend into the stone. You walk the slippery slope into the belly of the cave. Bats screech in the vast alcoves above. You walk. You slip. You continue walking for what seems like days. Just when you feel confused as to your way through the stalagmites and stalactites, the stone seems to be more carved here. Stone steps have been carved into the coming floor. You take the steps carefully and descend further. You shiver in the damp cool and despair as to finding what it is you seem to be searching for. You make it to the lowest level of the cave and step down from the last step. A huge throne room expands in from of you. It is a large flat room with a stone dais a few paces away. Unseen torches light as you walk toward the throne. You are called to rest, so you kneel on the steps. She is here. She is hearing your prayers. You feel her hand on your bowed head.

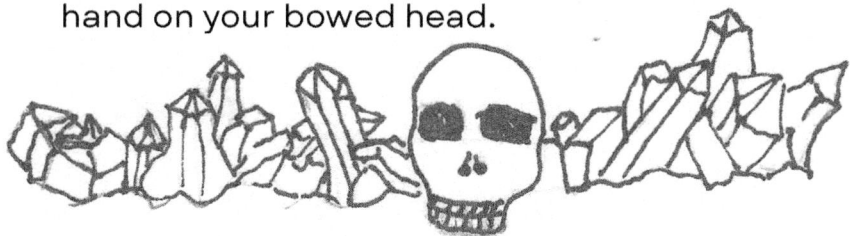

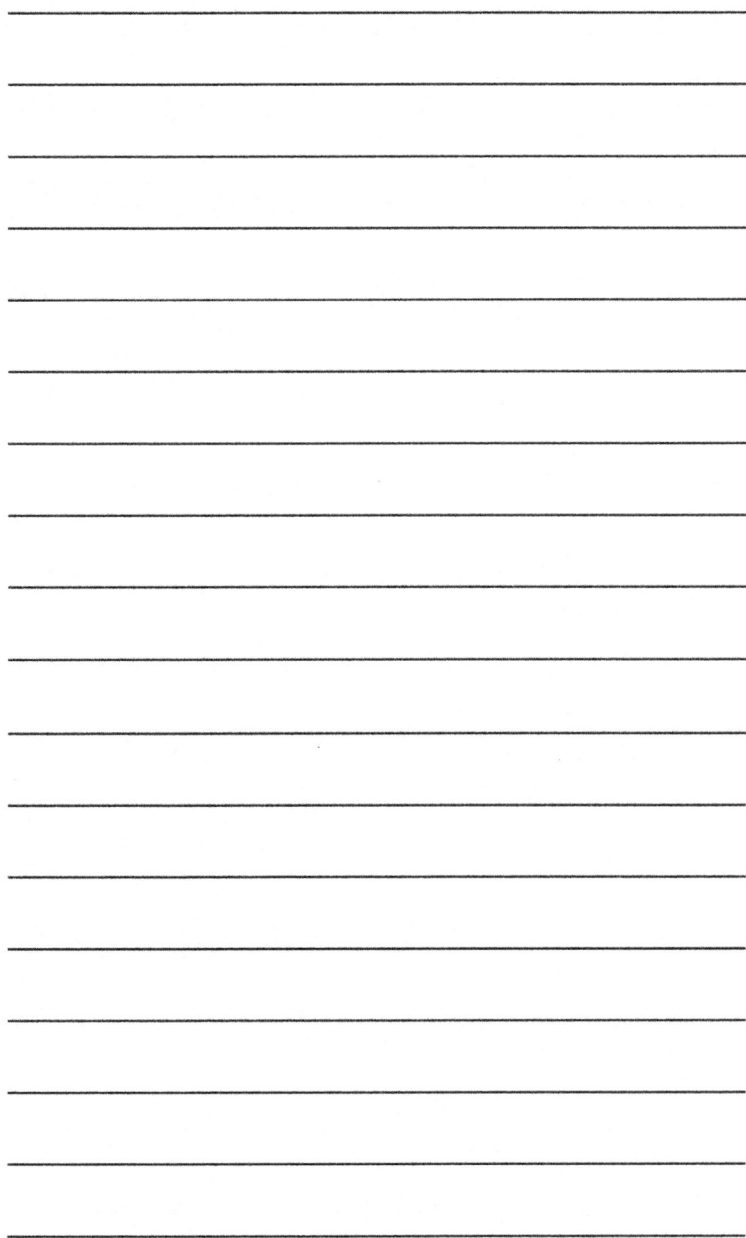

Persephone

Dread Persephone

I See You Standing There, Backlit By Hell
Holding Wildflowers In Your Hand.
Thousands Of Enmities In Your Hair Waft
Curling Rays Swaying In The Heat.
With Every Downward Step, You Demand
Respect From Those In These Realms.
Feeling Into Your Duality, I See Your Aspects
Reflected In your Glowing Eyes.
Your Breath Leaves Spring In Its Wake,
Caressing The Winds Of This Place.
You Don't Need To Carry A Scythe To
Command The Unnumerable Dead.
How Goes The Kingdom That Didn't Know
You Were Needed To Fulfil Their Veneration?

Queen of the Underworld

Congregate Mighty Dead,
Standing As My Army
In Eternal Resting,
For This, The Queen Of The Underworld.
Shift Spirits As One Whole,
We Are Not The Sum Of Our Parts.
The Power Is Palpable,
Felt Glory In The Groaning.
Dark Moon Rising Unseen,
Shaking New Chambers,
In The Hearts and In The Armors.
Lay Waste To Wild Becoming,
Wreckages From Hellfire Scour
Pavements Glistening With Inchor.
Bless The Stolen Mortalities,
Standing As My Army
In Internal Resting,
For This, The Queen Of Your Underworld.

Goddess of Flora

Kore–
Maiden Fair In Spring's
Meadow
Narcissus Adore To Be
Plucked
For Your Scented
Pleasure–
Oblivious To The
Lonely
Underworldly
Magnetism's Gaze.
Sleep Here In
Afternoon Sun Ripe
With Your
Pheromones Dusting
Forth The Chasm With
Which He'll Come To
Call Upon–
Dragged Through
Darkness You Cast A
Spell On The Blossom
Still In Your Hand
A Seed With Which
You Are Bound
By The Juice Dripping
From Your Lips

Our Descending Virgin

Wreathed In Descensions Dripping
From Slick Slits Templed In Radiant Grace
Plucking Cedars From Boughs
Cast Into Flame Of Divine Loves

Come What May
Winters Laden With Decaying
Dormancy Chewing The Sun
Vaults Be The Heights Released

Bleeding As Spirit Wafts
Across Frigid Breaths From Warm Mouths
Powering The Interference Cycles
Dying Roses Petaled In Offering

Coined In Gold Branches Fraught
With Laden Fruit Clutched Ripe Roots
Drawing Sigils In Sea Sands
Offer Bliss To Autumns And Springs

Bountiful Princess

Abundant Princess
Sitting Placid In Grain
Loving The Spring
Due Flowers Can't Contain

Come Forth From Mother
Seeding Ground We Stand
A Gentle Worker
Willing To Lay A Hand

Coming Autumn
He Calls From Beneath
Angering Vegetation's Growth
With The Land Heath

Doting Princess
Answer The Summons
For When Spring Comes Again
You'll Bring Back The Sun

Infernal Shadowess

Darkness Calls For You,
Infernal Shadowess.
Like Rum Cakes Settling On Cool Windows
As The Mist Conjures Ghosts;
Singing In Graveyards
Waiting On The Flames Of Lover's Dalliance.
Shadowess Reminding You,
Infernal Darkness,
Feral Calls Like Howling In Moonlight
As Abandoned Woods Left Forgotten,
Dirt Roads Laid Out
Leading You Back To Hades.

Bride of Death

With Your Beauty And Grace

You Never Had A Chance.

Caught The Eyes Of Hell

And Its Throned Inhabitant.

He Set You Upon His Lap

Made Vows Between The Seeds

Let You Roam Where You Must

Seeing To Your Every Need.

Whispering Among The Dead

He'll Love You Evermore.

With Sweet Eternal Surrenders

Together You'll Rule

THE UNDERWORLD.

Witch of Promises

Vow Kissed On Brows

Of Satan's Dream

Pearlescent Survival

Pledged To Souls

One Trajectory Mind's Eye

Oath Taken Eternally Damned

Asserting Decaying Spells

Craft Promises Warrant Addicts

Consecrate The Holy Communion

Of Witches Cursing

Fingers Crossed Along Backs

Of Those Who Will Dwell

In Satan's Slumbering

Demanding Pinkie Bones Rent

Spent Devotions Monarch

Read Incantations Aloud

To Wishes Cast On Candle Flames

Affirming Nether Pits Fuming

Condemned With Your Sworn

Equinox Empress

And In The Vanishing Light Of Autumn
Descend—
Your Essence With Leaves
As Brown As The Mud
Soft Impact With The Dying Of The Sun
Back, Back, Back To Colder Caves
To Embraces Tucked Around The Fires Of Hell
The Immortality Of Death's Reign
Joyful Tears As Snowflakes
Melt On Your Cheeks Warmed From The
Seasons Crowding In Your Breast

And With The Taste Of Spring's Kiss
Ascend—
Your Essence With Lush
As Green As Grass Blades
Soft Impact With The Coming Of The Sun
Back, Back, Back To Warmer Climbs
To Embraces Full Of Nostalgic Memories
The Immortality Of Life's Reign
Joyful Tears As Raindrops
Chilled On Your Cheeks Frozen From The
Seasons Pressing In Your Breast

Mother of Mortals

Feed The Dead From Your Breast
Oh, Mother Of Mortals
Bosom Warm With Hugging Light
Left Over From Spring Clocks
Walking Toward Hell's Children
Groaning For Your Compassion
Skeleton Form Nurseries
Nests Built From Methane Gas
Rose Garden Nurtured In
Abyss We Call Our Immortal Home
Sack Lunches For Picnics Along River Styx
Sing Out A Lullaby Of Souls
Calling From
Voids Undetectable To Loving Ears
Oh, Mother Of Mortals

Charmer of Beasts

Charmer Of Beasts,

Your Demons On A Leash,

Scorn To Never Cease,

Should You Ever Release.

Liminal Liaison

Plant Flowers At The Graves
Of The Selves That Are
Untransformed,
Standing In Doorways,
Lost To The Liminal Fog.
Pull Me Forward, Backward,
Liminal Liaison,
One Way Out, Through.
Risk Of Bondage To The Creatures
Who Wish Selves To Stay.
Teach Liminal Listening
So That When Emerging
Implement What They Have Known

Necromanceress

Dig Me Up, Dig Me Down
Take Care Of My Soul
Don't Leave Me In The Ground
Take Me To Your Domain
Rob My Mortal Grave
With You I Will Remain
(x3)

Consort of Katabasis

Journey Down To Dwelling's Rot

Retrieve Immortality Forsaken Me

Lost Mirrors That No Longer Reflect

Vital Wisdom Shared In The Descent

Distance In Days, Months, Years

Fall With Me Gentle Maiden

Open The Chasms With Secret Words

Riding The Crevasse Across Tundra

Spirit Beasts Come Fetch Me

Attracted To Sacrificial Bloods

Where The Sun Is Silent

Consorting With Abandon's Wrath

Lust Be For The Trodden

Down To Dark Netherworlds

Everlasting Underworld's Fumes

Drink From Celestial Southern Bowl

Enter The Darkened Path

Drunken In Caves Made For You

TEMPLE OF SCARLET SEEDS

Awaken in a lush meadow. Autumn florals are blooming in all directions. It smells like earthly decay and sunburnt leaves. You stand and look around to the surrounding trees currently going through their autumnal release. Leaves are rustling underfoot in the wind. Off in the distance, you notice a stone gazebo folly. It seems to be lit from within and with a rush of excitement, you trek through the crushing leaves towards this columned temple. You step up a couple of steps to stand inside this pavilion. A sweet smell wafts towards you and you look across this folly. You walk to a pomegranate tree holding vigil right outside. You pick the best one, pluck it and rip it open with your bare hands. Going back to the folly, you sprinkle the scarlet seeds on the floors. As you do, you feel her, a soft thank you.

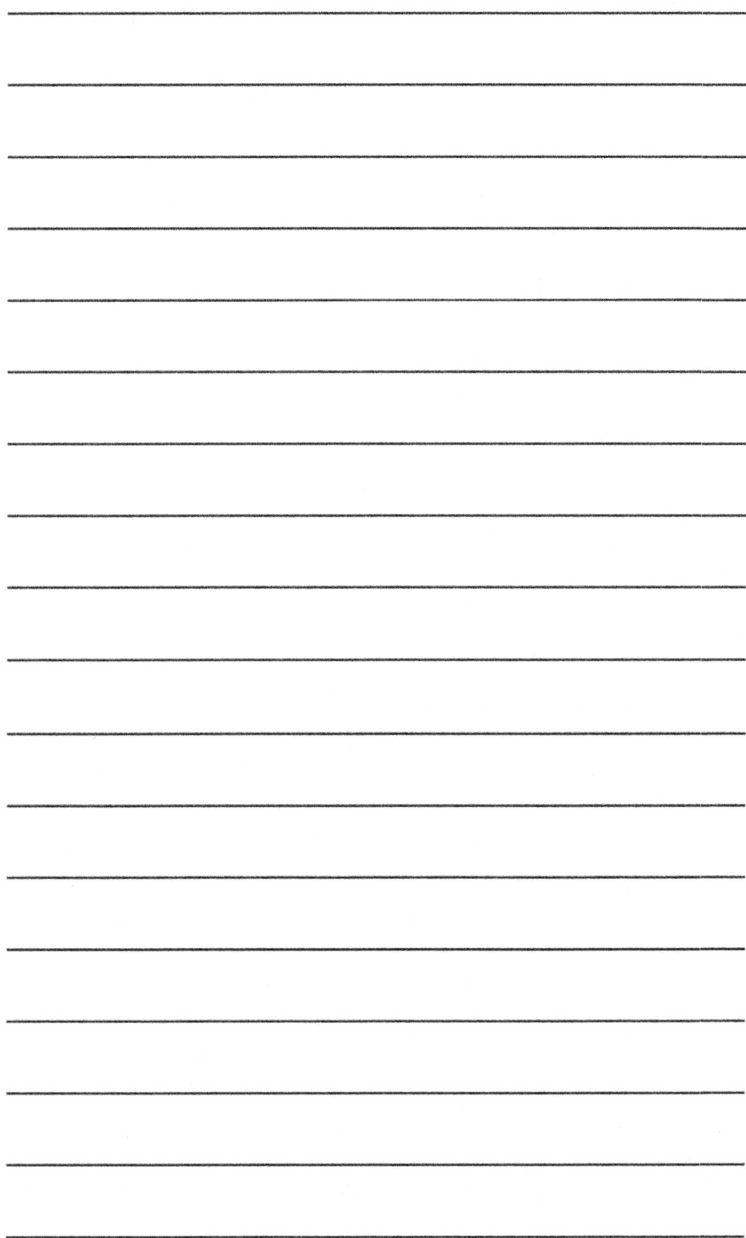

Lilith

Seductress of the Soulless

Obsidian-Eyed Seductress
Suck The Souls Through Crimson Lips

Tongues Trapped in Teeth
Rotten in Fanged Lust
Cast Be The Bones
Thrown Over Writhing Limbs
Touch Free The Wanton Dominion
Honey Drenched Paths
Contacted By Silver Coins
Travel Underworld Precipices
Fallen Be The Stars
You Are Made From
Seduce Charmers of Ego
Bite Around Bared Necks
Cloaked In Driven Hubris

Obsidian-Eyed Seductress
Suck The Souls Through Crimson Lips

Satirical Succubus

Plunder The Sheaths
I, Succubus Of Creation
Not Here To Fulfil
Your Raw Expectations

Strip The Skins
I, Succubus Of Conception
Not Here To Conform
Your Vile Situations

Rob The Nodes
I, Succubus Of Production
Not Here To Please
Your Depraved Satisfactions

Steal The Armor
I, Succubus Of Suction
Not Here To Suit
Your Lewd Imagination

Demoness

What Terrifying
Attraction
Of The Demoness'
Vile Stings.

What Alarming
Allure
Of The Demoness'
Cursed Wings.

What Grim
Bait
Of The Demoness'
Ghastly Cling.

What Lurid
Fright
Of The Demoness'
Spectral Springs.

What Dim
Trap
Of The Demoness'
Vast Everything.

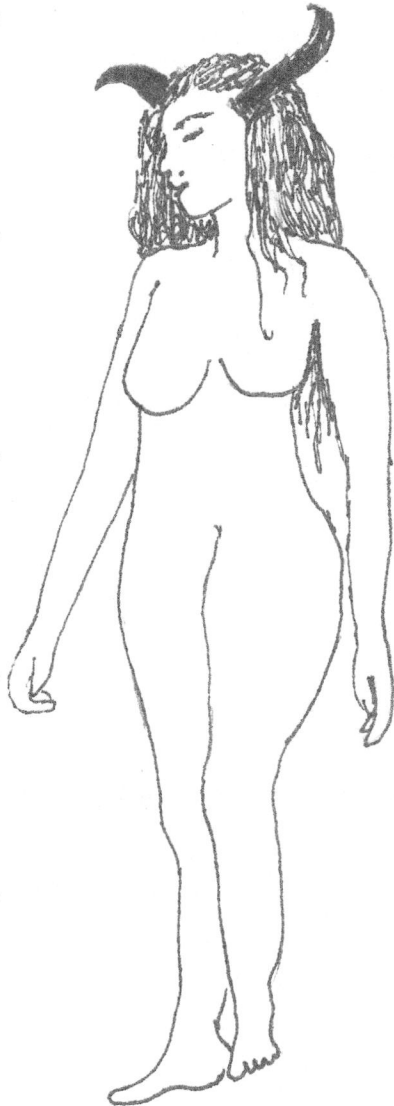

Our Lady Of The Rejected

Our Lady Of The Rejected!

Oh, Immoral One.
Oh, Rejected One.
Have Mercy On Our Heavy Hearts
Cast Out From Divine's Thrall.

Covered In Shame And Guilt
Let Not Out Thoughts
Become Out Bower.

Cast In Sanctimonious Dark
Let Not Our Mistakes
Transform Who We Are.

Our Lady Of The Rejected!

Oh, Immoral One.
Oh, Rejected One.
Have Mercy On Our Burdened Souls
Forsaken By Divine's Light.

Outcast Siren

Paradise Fashioned From Dying Roses
In the Garden Of Paradox.

Slice Thighs With Thorns
Slick With Pleasure's Wings.

Dew Bejeweled Grounds
Honeyed Lips Moan The Sunrises.

Handle With Delicate Cares
Rewrite Sordid Tales Of The Outcast.

Cry Forth Maroon Petals
Twirl The Siren Dance.

Screaming Into Furled Voids
Lubricate Exposed Red Skies.

Dry Siphoned Perfume Of Dying Roses
In The Garden Of Paradox.

Harlot of the Kingdom

Infernal Harlot Made From Hate
They Know You Not
You're Their Escape.

Unjust Conformity Of Wills
For Not Your Own
Take Your Thrills.

Desirous Madam Thy Self Be True
Even In Dominance
Command The Clues.

Kingdoms Fallen Over Thrones
Process The Battlefields
You Need Not Atone.

Damned Wonders Of Savagery
They Hold Out Hope
You Will Not Marry.

Ghastly Maiden Created From Cruelty
Take Your Placed Stance
You Of Vast Duty.

Queen of the Possessed

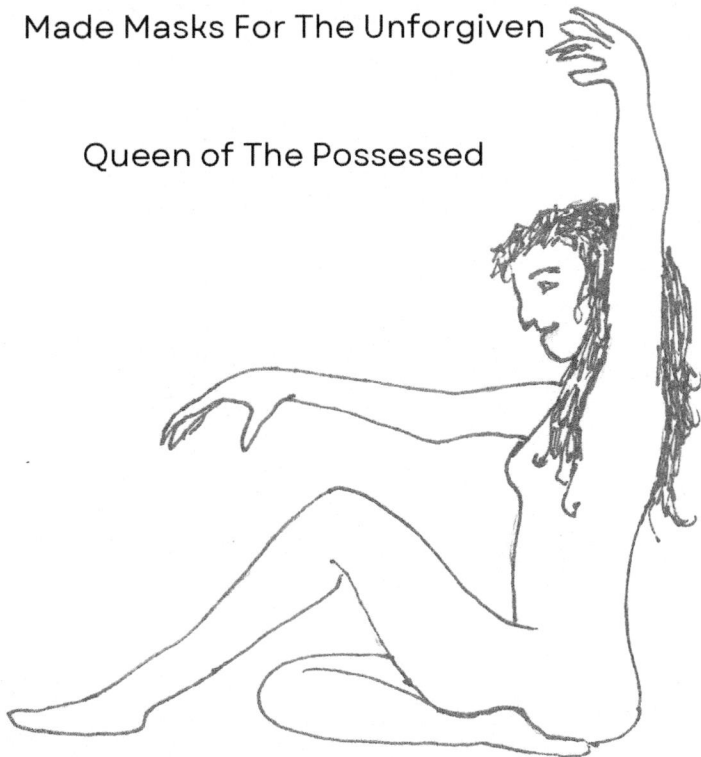

Tangled Possessive Needs Shift Great

Conjure Familiar Strife Conjecture

Cradle Thief Of Undue Circumstances

Changeling Switches At Gleaming Altars

Lovers At Varied Slithering Helms

Greedy Rituals With Vaporous Spirits

Soaked In Ectoplasmic Bloodlust

Made Masks For The Unforgiven

Queen of The Possessed

First Woman

First Woman Of Creation

Just In The Wandering

Submission Not Required

Cured Of Ails

Cursed Dire Straits

Alarming Those Who Dwell

Hereto Under Rotten Bodies

Brave First Woman

Cast Aside For Uniformity

Choke On Angel's Smoke

Merging With Raw Power

Sit A Spell Of Potencies

No Lament For The Wickedless

Devouress

Devouress
Devouress

Suffice It To Say
You Mastered The Rebellion.
Lie Among The Tired Tears
Of Heavens War.
Shove Through Won Victories
Around The Devouring Essences
In Loosened Fervor.
Terminate And Create Nuance
For The Half Eaten Flesh.
Absorb Dispatched Web Clasps.
Experience Futile Debauch Justices.
Describe Further Longings
Of Voracious Histories.

Devouress
Devouress

Dominatrix of Vast Dominions

Slick Leather, Damp With Decaying

Pleasures.

Rot Away The Layers Of Skin, Use As

Whips. Lounging Corpses Abound The

Circumference Of Your Domain.

Holler To The Dead.

Honor To The Dead.

Ball-gag The Next Victim Of Death.

Make Them Cry With Glorious

Gratification.

Make Them Beg In Your Name.

Cast Them To The Red Walls.

Await A New Sacrifice In Leather Slick

With Pleasure's Decay.

Vampiress

Summon Forth Vampiress
Drain The Vitality
Siphon Cold Hearts
Funnel Dread Existence
Channel Impulsive Zests
Sieve Dried Souls
(x3)

Vengeful Vixen

Vengeful Vixen
You Who Knows No Sin

Captivating Magnetic Pull
Drink The Blood
Tastes Of Dark Chocolate
Fall Down To Red Velvet
Glamour Soaked In Leathers
Entice The Hate Filled Memories
Penetrate With Your Horns
Choregraph Devilish Dances
Charm The Sweat From Brows
Lick The Salty Wounds
Suck Dry The Poisoned Vessels
Forth Be To Your Slick
Quivering In Every Wake

Witch of the Rapture

Peeling Judgments Of Pearl Walls

Cast Down From Those Vast Halls.

Locked Away From Prying Hands

Cruelest Witch In All The Lands.

Silenced and Alone You Be

Shuttered From The World Of Greed.

When The Rapture Comes Along

Your Heart Will Beat Ever Strong.

Witch Of The Fallen And Condemned

You Will Never Meet Your End.

Irreverent One

Guttural Groans Know The Causality

Of Blind Ecstasies In Your Wonder.

Uncontained and Unrestrained.

Sovereign Of Prideful Defiance

Hissing Caustic Of Autonomous Ends.

Seize Mirrored Vanities

In Callous Capricious Rituals.

Sweet Aromas Of Darkened Abodes.

Call Forth The Just Indignations

Of Pure Naysayers.

Take Fight To Irreverent Sand

Dunes Under The Dark Moon.

Rot Complacent Chime Droning

Lounging Languid Dank Lacquered Floors.

Brand Crescents On Bared Breasts

Dripping Noxious Swill.

TEMPLE OF TANTALIZED NEED

A sheer red curtain awaits you. It shifts eerily in the stifling heat. Lifting your hand, you separate the sheers in hopes to get a glimpse of the opulence. A wall of dragon's blood incense hits you. It makes you hazy, lulled. In the delicate state between awake and asleep, you make you way into a small room. Maroon rugs line the floor. You are mesmerized by their shapes and intricate stitches.

She's here. You can sense Her. Plumes of smoke waft about, sinking your head into unclear thoughts and feelings.

You walk along, feet silent.

You trip on a floor pillow. No fear. Nothing. Just bliss as you fall.

You land softly on a mound of pillows that has been waiting on you.

Here you linger, basking in glorious sensations.

Here, you just need.

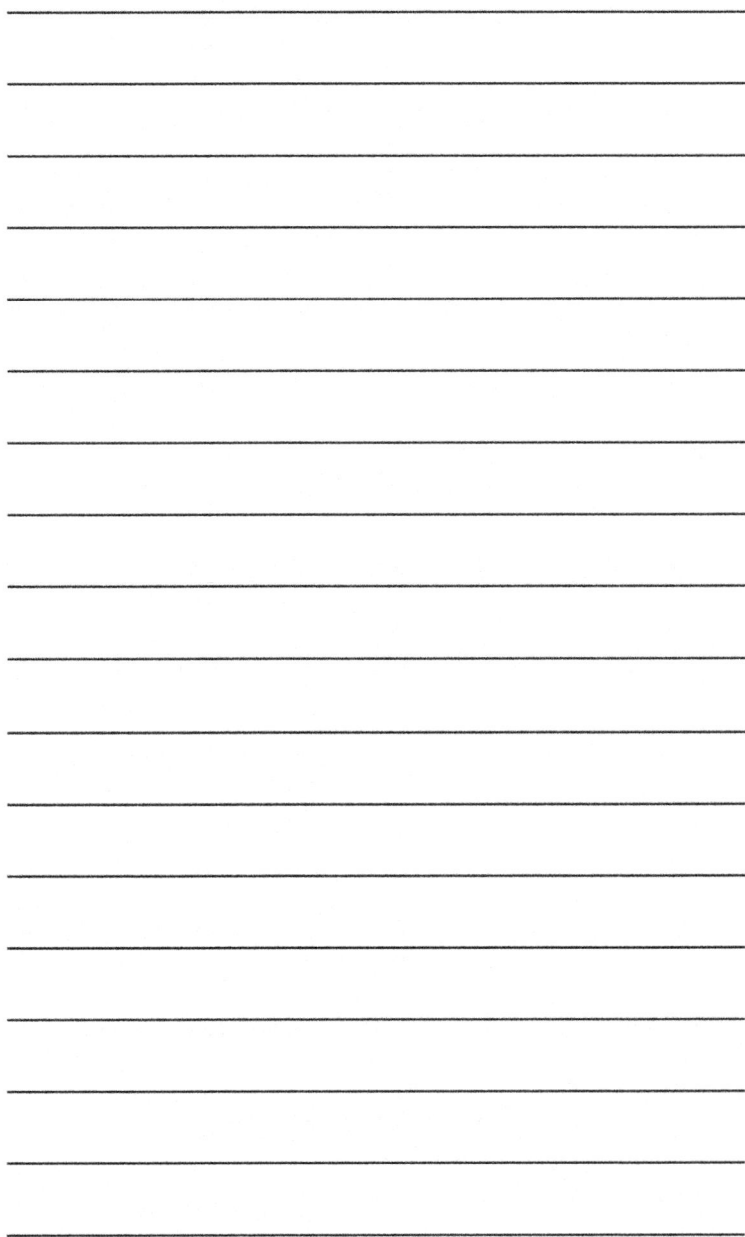

Cailleach

Hag of Winter

O, Hag Of Winter,
Blossom Us Into Snow Angels
Made From The Laughter Of Season's Long
Gone.
Hush Be The Coming Dark.
Pray For Sustaining Sustenance
For All Under You Pitiful Skies.

O, Hag Of Winter,
Mold Us Into Snowflakes
Made From The Tears Of Season's Long
Gone.
Quiet Be The Coming Chill.
Pray For Comforting Coziness
For All Under Your Poor Lands.

O, Hag Of Winter,
Carve Us Into Long Icicles
Made From The Salts Of Season's Long
Gone.
Silent Be The Coming Frost.
Pray For Soothing Synapses
For All Under Your Dismal Season.

Blower of the North Winds

North Winds

Cometh

On The Back Of Autumn.

Reaper Grants A Scythe...

Blow Up The Winds

Of Change

Zephyr Forth From Earth's Pole

Northern Lights Did Mask

The Magnetic Beasts

Of Soul Foods

Crone of Chill

Slip Sick Within Winter's Chill
Harboring Snowflakes In Your Covered
Shawl.
Let To Die In Colder Stills
Basking Sunlight In Your Cascading Winter's
Brawl.

Woman Of Blight

Unfurl The Gusts

Of Blight Upon The Lands

Lay Waste To Growths

Only You Command

Cry Out Crazy

This Season Of Blight

Protected In The Cocoon

Of Winter's Bite

Ban In The Womb

Of Hibernation's Warmth

Play The Music Of Snow

In Your Fine Form

Great Weather Grandmother

Great Weather Grandmother,
Teach Us The Old Ways.
As We Settle In
Clinging To Autumn Too Closely
You Blow Forth Your Wisdoms.

Great Weather Grandmother,
Teach Us The Old Ways.
As We Settle In
Holding Dead Leaves Too Closely
You Blow Forth Your Wisdoms.

Great Weather Grandmother
Teach Us The Old Ways.
As We Settle In
Holding Wilting Flowers Too Closely
You Blow Forth Your Wisdoms.

As We Wish For Spring On Every Star,
Teach Us The Power Of Nature,
Great Weather Grandmother.

Giantess

Your Body As The Mountain
Your Breath The Low-Hanging Clouds
Blowing Hair As The Strong Trees
Fingers As The Hilly Mounds

Your Feet Are The Oceans
Your Arms Shake The Tides
Shoulders Mold The Canyons
Thighs Are The Rivers That Collide

Your Dress Is The Blanket Of Snow
Their Flakes Come From Your Eyes
Your Teeth Are Ancient Cairns
Your Mouth Is Where The Sun Will Rise

Lightning Sculptor of Mountains

Conjure The Lightning From The Sky
Crack It On Unshakeable Grounds
Mold The Mountains In Their Wake.

Harsh Hag Halting

Harsh Hag Halting

Bitter Bleak Bold

Corporeal Coarse Cold

Sinister Slaking Slow

Shielded Shearing Soul

Crass Crude Chapped

Bawdy Boorish Blue

Hard Horrific Hoarse

Barbaric Blue Face

Barbaric Blue Face
Aware Of Winter's Coming.
Spirited Winds In Darling Freezes
Last Season's Drumming.
(x3)

Blustering One

You May Be The Blustering One
But There Is Fire In Your Soul
The Many Hands Of Winter Comes
Everything Is In Nature's Control

You Blanket The Seeds Sown
An Upside Down Circulation
Necessary For Vegetation
Fusing Its Percolation

The Winds Are Blowing Now
Coming In From Your Hot Breaths
Chief Of The Colder Climates
Nature Will Put Us Through The Test

Veiled Virago

Bad-Tempered Woman,

Under The Veil Of Winter,

Chilled To Her Old Bones,

Quaking In Rotting Valleys.

Render Me Unworthy

Of The Wheel That Turns

While Winter Is So Still.

The Bell Toles At Midnight

On A Lingering Solstice.

Thunderess

Thundress Moaning

In Valleys All But Lost—

Take Back The Swallowing Grace

Of Harvest's Release.

Falling Like The Leaves

Leaving Behind Warmer Weathers

Swirling On The Cusp Of

Harsher Colds—

Fever Racking Coughs Up Bloods

Of Ancient Prophecies Rendered From

Crones Long Since Passed.

Listening—

Boulder Wielder

Wield The Boulders

Against Cold Shoulders

Ever Getting Older

Mountain Molder

The Winter Upholder

Glacier Polder

Storm Roller

Nothing Smoldered

North And South Polar

Midwife of Dormant Seeds

Seeds Going Dormant
In Your Bitter Breaths
No Bounty To Be Found
We Offered What Was Left

Take Us Into Strange Arms
Let Us Suckle On The Peak
If Not, We May Not Survive
Rendering Springs Weak.

Coddle Us In Your Bosom
Don't Let Us Go Stray
The Winds Are Howling In Our Blood
In The Dying Light Of Day

Discipline Our Beloved Hearts
Nurse Us For The Winter
Careful Sow From Seasons Past
Demolish All Who May Enter

Storm Summoner

Dreamy In Winter's Reveries

Vortices Echoing Along The White Pelts Of

Chilling Air.

Clouds Rolling In From Your Dark Days

Mountainous Retreat.

Thunder Before Lightnings Blasts.

In Your Eyes, Tears Of Snow Fall Down Into

Lochs Of Ancient Ages.

Storm Is Brewing In Your Cauldrons Ringing

Resonances Sounding Fallen.

Wishing On Dead Tree Branches Shelters

Erected In Summer's Haze.

TEMPLE OF FROZEN BREATHS

You awaken on the peak of a large mountain. The air is thin up here and it is freezing cold. You shiver on your back. Judging on the clouds, the sky, and the sun, it is midmorning. You stand and look down at a great valley slowly receiving the sun. You look up and spin around, raise your arms. You are utterly alone here. Stand for hours on her precipice. The sun meets you up here at the summit at noon. As you chant a winter ballad on the wind, clouds pass the mountain and it begins to snow. You feel her in these snowflakes falling on your cold cheeks. She is melting on your upturned face along with your reverent tears.

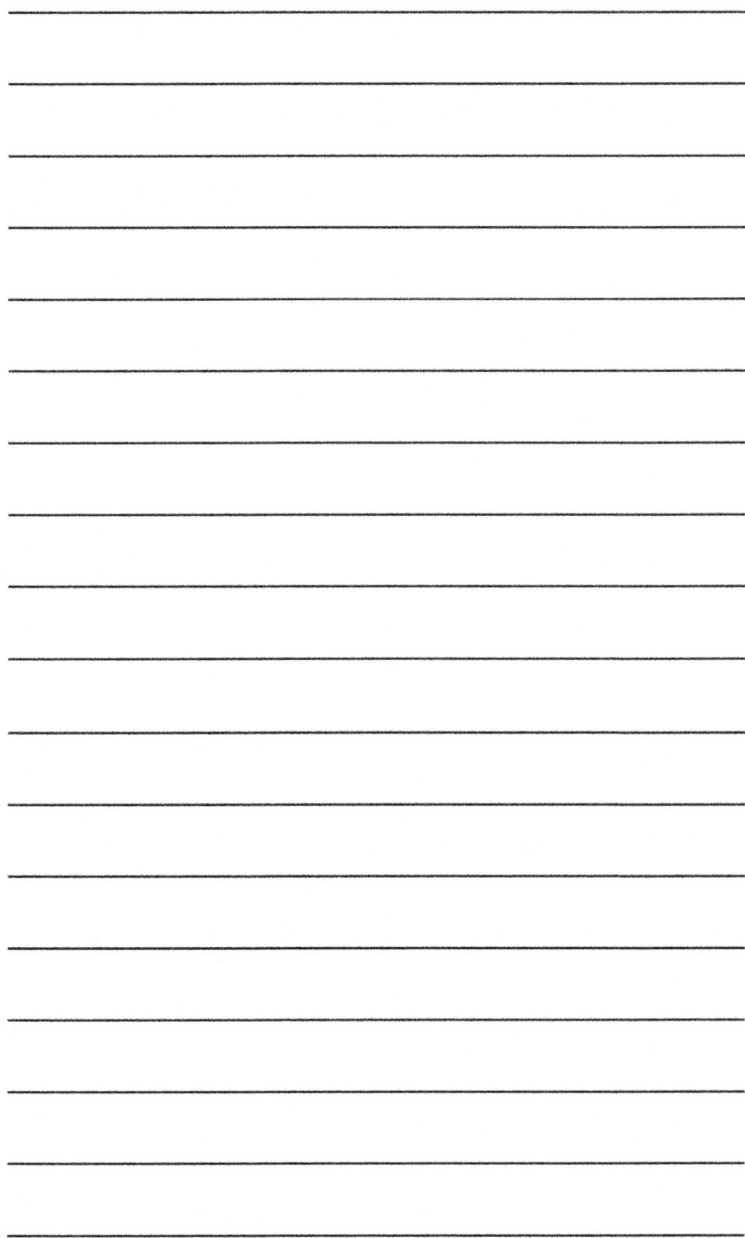

Baba Yaga

Hag of the Glade

Wandering In Sweet Twilight
A Moonlit Glade Awakens
A Screech Of An Owl Hoots Overhead.
Dangling Branches Scratch Pink Cheeks
In The Winds Of Night.
Baba, Baba, Bubushka.
I Call To You, Grandmother.
Help Me. Help Me.
Help Me Find My Way.
Flicking Lights Appear, Floating On Air.
Dark Laughter Haunts This Place
And I Am Far From Home.
Crying To Be So Near,
I Walk Towards The Smell Of Baking Bread.
Locked From You, In This Liminal Place,
I Stand At Your Skull Gate, Waiting.
Please, Let Me In.
Hag Of This Glade.
Softly Did The Creak Of Hinges Sound.
I Made It Safely To You,
Now, Please, Open Your Door.
Baba, Baba, Babushka.

Wood Sap Grandmother

Howling In The Night
Prowling The Dark Forest Canopy.
Find An Old Oak
And Mind His Time Finally.

Dripping That Sweet Balm
Sipping That Sweet Dew.
The Wood Sap Is Clean
It Is Birthing Anew.

Should You Poke Around
It Will Cures All Ills.
Bite From The Trunk
Sure To Get Your Fill.

Cackler of Trees

Cackle Up The Woods,
For All Who Never Understood.
The Righteous And Good.
Blast Be Those Who Could.
Reverent To Those Who Should.
(x3)

Teacher in the Thicket

Teach Us The Bramble Stroke

That Of The Briar

Stabilize Thickets Of Forests' Damp Floors

Support Nature's Way Of Covering Us With

Her Grace.

Accept Various Challenge The Wood Brings

In The Scab And Spring—

In The Harvest Opportunity.

Strength Of Heart In Coming Winter's Kiss.

The Wood World Is Hard.

You're The Voice Of Experiencing The

Canopy Wide Overhead.

Understanding Brings Your Harsh Cut Upon A

A Bush Dame's Lip.

Track Prints Covered In Mud and Sticks.

Knowing Knowledge Welds And Melds

Earthen Wisdoms Rotting Bringing

Mushrooms To Our Tables.

Elder Of The Hollar

Elder Of The Hollar

Work.

For Life Means Labor

Maintain The Valley In Between The

Mountain.

Call Upon The Power Of The Trees,

For There Are Ages Inside Them.

Building Community Inside The Forests

Conversations.

Open The Doors, Unlock Sacred Dappled

Sunlight.

Share The Earth With All.

Witch of the Wind Between The Trees

The Wind Between The Trees Is Forgotten By
Humans Rushing Towards Progress.

The Witch Makes Her Home There,
Caught With The Wind In The Boundaries.

Her Gifts Are Branchy Birch Hands,
Gnarled From The Bark Of All Trees.

Loving Acts Of Throwing Seeds To Those
Who Dwell In This Vast Forest.

Get Things Done Within The Hours Of
Daylights Fanciful Germinations.

Rewards Be To Those Who Find Solace In
These Places, Boons Await.

Find This Wind Witch Of The Forest,
Get Out There And Walk The Sacred Road.

Never Forget That Life Is A Journey,
And The Wind Is A Gift.

Warden of the Wildwood

Between The Margins,
Making Hard Bargains.
There In Lonesome Trees,
Demanding We Say Please.
(x3)

Wielder of the Wakeful Flame

When All Is Lost
I Look For You
In The Ever Darkening Forest.
Careful In Your Hut
Impossible Tasks Ensued
I Carry Out Your Warrants.

By Stepping Up
You Set Me Right
For I Was Wandering Adrift.
Hollering To My Face
You Will Heal
While I Am In Your Midst.

When All Is Complete
I Stand Accomplished
You Sing Me A Dark Lull.
Kiss Me On My Cheek
Send Me On Home
With A Talismans Of Skulls.

Feral Farer

Faring On In Feral Glory
Taking The Forest's Inventory.
Journeying Across The Wood
In A Mortar There You Stood.
Up You Fly With Pestle In Hand
Ever Watchful Of The Land.

(x3)

Guardian of the Woodland Path

Kneel On The Forest Floor
Security Bleeds And Fixes The Core.

The Guardian Will Come
Transformed You Will Become.

Shaken By Opening Surrounds
Noise Of The Woods Abounds.

Stop Before You Meander
And Smell The Flora And Gander.

Fix Your Eyes Upon The Structure
Careful At This Forest Juncture.

Ready To Always Defend
The Forests Need Your Mend.

Your Path May Twist
But You As A Spirit Exists.

Take Heed Your Inner Limiting
Even If You're Only Visiting.

Feast Upon The Edges
Pay Attention To The Hedges.

The Forest Is All Inescapable
But You Will Stand Unshakeable.

The Untamed One

Acrimonious And Untamed,

Like The Melting Sun

Or The Cool Rivers Running Underfoot.

All Is Covered Except Your Feet.

With A Besom In Your Hand, You Glare.

Across The Forest, You Seek All Who

Wanders

Searching Out The Lost Souls.

Say Their Names On The Breezes.

Catch Them In Their Darkest Hours.

Lure Them With Smells Of Home,

So Far From Their Center.

Dance A Jig Upon Your Merry Lawn,

And Wait.

Here One Comes Now.

Benefactor of the Backwood

Poppies Surround The Gate
Of The Benefactor Of The Backwood.

A Sign There Reads

"eye for an eye,
tooth for a tooth.
if they ache you
ill pull 'em out by the root."

Ogress Of The Oaks

There's Lightning Bugs In Her Spine
This Keeper Of The Acorns

Devotion Renders Her Imperative
In The Ritual Opening Spaces

Forests' Heart Thrums In Her Chest
Beats Quick As A Hummingbird

Swallowing Monster Magic
In Her Hungry Gaping Maw

Take A Bite Out Of The Barks
Chunks Regurgitate In Dew

Standing Never Idle In Moonlight
Manifesting Shrapnel In Her Veins

Tools In The Shed Of The Mind
She Has Given All She Is

Wilderness Wanderer

Forbidden Footsteps Transform
The Hollow Savior's Lots

Soaked Powerful Forces Move
Within The Wilderness

Irreducible In Their Power
When The Machine Comes

Matter Turns Soft In Rains
Slowly Making It To Duffs

Loses Touch With Outsides
Cosmos In The Towering Pines

Glimpse Her Worlds Within
The Brittle Breath Of Wilderness

Harpy of Unsated Hunger

Harpy Of Unsated Hunger
Eating My Rotten Memories.
Devour All That Needs To Go
Leave No Room For Remedies.
Harpy Of Unsated Hunger
Eating My Decayed Flesh.
Swallow All That Needs To Go
Make Me New And Fresh.
(x3)

TEMPLE OF HUMMING PINES

Awaken, lying in lush grass, on the edge of a vast forest. Nothing but trees as far as the eyes can see. The sun is dying in the west. A path leads inward. Scared, but resolute, you stand and place one foot in front of the other. The forest grows denser as you tread. Saplings then have now grown into large oaks and pines. They're humming, sharing. The light has deserted you here. However, fickle flames dance in your periphery. You cast this your new direction. You come upon a gate made of skull lanterns. Encircling what you can barely make out. A hut! Chicken legs brace this tiny abode. Walk the pebble path to the door.
Knock!

Medusa

Pythoness

Penetrating, Piercing
Ssssockets Of Holy
Transformation.
I Be But A Hair
On Your Head.
Writhing And Slithering
Split Tongue Not Speak
To Whom On Your Path.
Ssscale For Ssscale
Liminal Priestessss
Once Ensconced.
Through Wet Grassses.
May I Be Ssssick
And Fall Ssslowly
To Tread On Belliesss.
Hail Pythoness!
Hail Pythonesssss!

Monstress

Wretched Visage Scares
In Demonic Stares Given To You
From Vengeful Goddess
Aimless Clapping Of Bitten
Hairs That Tear Away
Sensical Laughs At The
Sensible Hate Filled Nights
Inside Inner Sanctums
Arrogant With Distaining
Buttons Fastening Master Cloaks
With Binders Of Clay
Wait For Another Dawn

Conjurer of Immobility

Conjure The Dust
Up From The Footfalls
Of Those Who Would Corrupt
Sick Sedition Playing
Wreaking Havocs Degradation

Contaminate The Dirt
Down From Modest Slides
Of Those Who Would Sully
Ravish Soil Molesting
Pollute Profanity Besmirchment

Conjure The Ashes
Down From Tarnished Faults
Of Those Who Would Deface
Pillage Hurt Immobilizing
Destroy Foul Dishonourment

Witch Of Petrifying Gaze

Come Around The Corner!
Ye, Of Pathetic Mourners.
Bring You Into The Light
Let Me See You, Despite
I May Grant Mercy
You Should Only Hurry
Drop Your Mirror Hither
*Oh, Will You Wither
Take In My Dress
Making Striding Progress
Now Gaze Into My Eyes
Fire Burning From Inside
Turn To Stone Before Me
Not Even On Your Knees
Statues From All Tests
Forever Shall You Rest
Stand Firm In This Lair
Guarding With Blank Stares
Though Victims In This Event
I Bore The Full Extent

Venomous Priestess

Sanctuary Slain
Anguished Heart
Rise To Vessels
Adjunct To Oils
Spilling Fire
In Her Name
Take Pity For Fear
Above All Else
Fangs Descend
As Hair Falls
Where Snakes Now
Stand
Poisonous
Where Prizes Once
Were
Venomous Virgin
Forever More.

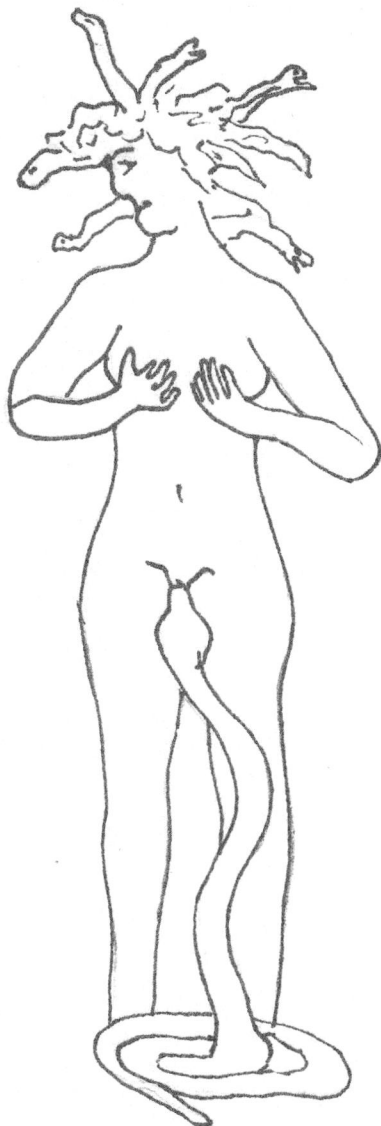

Sorceress Of The Shield

With Gifts From The Gods
Your Reflection Shown
Down You Went
To The Lair Unknown

Upon A Slumber Bed
Medusa Lay In Wait
Swish Goes Your Sword
Your Thrust Was Great

Of Perseus Did Sever
The Head Of The Gorgon
Her Death Was Swift
The Deed Not Undone

Head To The Shield
To War And To Success
Medusa Casts Her Glances
Now A Fearsome Sorceress

Our Lady of the Betrayed

Athena's Doom
Reigns Over Temples
Where Maidens
Lose What They Treasure

Athena's Wrath
Rings Clear Bells
Maidens Carry
Lost Captured Beauty

Athena's Jealousy
Rips Through Walls
Maidens Clean
Losing Their Care For

Courtesan of Curses

Courtesan Teaching Curses
To The Cursed
Where No Man Dare Tread

Deep In Sanctums
To Pardon The Lost
Stone Reflecting In Your Eyes

Cardinal Virtues Rise
For The Cursed
In Places No Man Will Go

Scold The Madness
Of Lustful Gods
Where Mortals Will Not Venture

Lady of Rightful Rage

Bind They Who Would Harm
Teach Through Your Disarm
With Dreadful Eyes That Charm
(x3)

The Mortal Gorgon

Mortal One Of Sisters Three

Cast Your Humanity

With Fallen Tusks

In Soft Meadows Where

The Blue Haired Man

Seafaring Await You

Sunlit In Loving Embraces

Lust Cresting Like Waves

Combing Fingers In Hair

Roped In Seaweed

Covering Your Shielded

Virgin Eyes Wandering

Over Watery Body

Entwined In Salty Tears

With Hymen Breaks

Impregnated With Wings

Stone Siren

To You I Pray
Show Me The Way
With Dazzling Gaze
Make Them Pay

(x3)

Mother Of Pegasus

Birth Horses With Wings

Flying Foals Conquering

Pearlescent Misty Skies Aloft

Pegasus

Stars Falling To Catch Up

Mystical Companion

To All Who Need Height

Pegasus

Rise From Temples

Lain Sacred With Snakes

Mothering Horses With Wings

Pegasus

Queen of the Shedding Skin

Shed your Skins

Raw With Power

To Soothe Violations

Take My Pain

Scalped In Despair

To Alleviate Darkness

Wracked With Abuse

Hiss Manic Beauty

To Heal Purity

Use All Your Eyes

Slither Over Corpses

To Conquer Love Lost

Sibyl of Scales

Oracle Of The Snake Skins
Caster Of Scales
Behold The Strewn Fortunes
On Valley Floors
Risks Taken For Messages
Tied To Cold-Bloodied Outcomes
Auguries In Crushed
Blades Of Green Grass
Intrigued In Writhing Whispers
The Serpent Twists It's Tail

Sibyl Of Scales
Look On To The Slithering Omens

TEMPLE OF HAUNTED STATUES

Awaken in a monstrous warehouse like building. You are standing among statues. Reverently running your fingers on a stone statue standing near you in this vast room of a hundred, thousands of others. You spin around and notice the poses, caught in a moment of life. They are stuck, forever remembering the gaze of Medusa. As you walk around, you caress each statue in your path.

Mindless, you begin to panic at the shear number of statues. You run, full speed in one direction. For seemingly miles, you run. Then, in another direction. You become lost. Just when you are lost among the stone, you feel Her. She's here, just around the next holy statues' expressionless gaze.

ALL HOLY IS HAUNTED

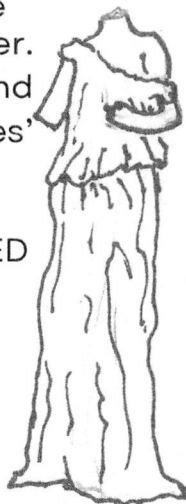

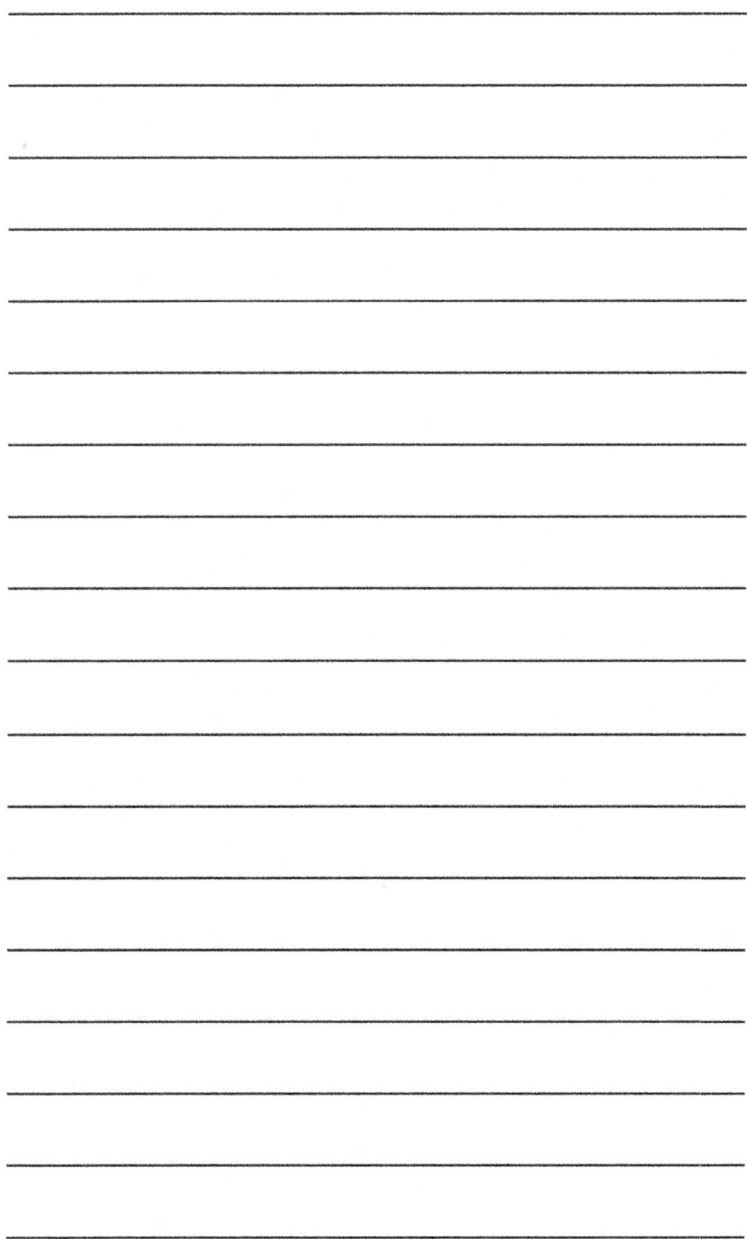

Medea

Princess of the Heartless

Princess of Colchis Fare
Follow Down
To Cold Stares
Malice Reigns
In Blackened Hearts
Vengeance Calls
For Its Depart
Flight Be to You
Of Heartless Bounds
Beat Only When
The Trumpet Sounds

Princess of Colchis Fare
Follow Down
In Dreaded Care
Rancor Stakes
On Darkened Doors
Should Hate Prevail
It Means War
Respect is Earned
In Empathic Intent
Careful Cinders
You Have Now Rent.

Sorceress of Sacrifices

Euphoric In You Martyrdom
Your Sacrifice Has Not Gone Unnoticed.
Success In Completely Histories.
You Own Your Casting Circles.
Dead Magics Streak Across The Skies
Shooting Down To Your Deeds.
Launch Your Lasting Defenses
Against The Crowds Of Conformity.
Sharp Focus On The Battlement
Directly Appeasing The Ones
On The Other End Of Magic.
Wind Around The Illuminated
Building Dreams Of All
What Might Be Left To Sacrifice.

Witch of Poisons

Make Your Poisons Deadly
Cold Whisking Flutters.
No Errors In Draught
Every Man Will Shudder.
(x3)

Enchantress of Magical Aid

Left For Wanting That Which

Calls For Magical Aid.

Celebrate The Pharmacia

In Your Laden Garden.

Pick From Concoctions

Remedies Best Served.

Under Eclipsed Suns,

Growth Cultivated From Magic.

Lasting Matrix Trough

In Hands Full Of Soil.

Water With Life Liquids

Flora To Gifting Radiance.

Share Success In Your

Comradery.

Daughter of Magic

Bestow Your Magics
Aiding The Failing Winds.
Conjure The Spell
For You Will Never Dim.
Calculate The Beating Heart
Radiating Forth From Your Hands.
Finding What Has Been Lost
Your Inner Golden Ram.

Maiden of Magnetism

Drifting About Your Penitence,
Lost To Your Destiny Roil.
You're Awakened By His Sparkled Eyes
But Know Him Not Too Much.
He Shines Ever Brightly.
You Didn't Know It Then,
But Battles Is All He Knows,
And Sweeping You Down Too
Laying Waste To Your Loves.
And—
Just When You're About To Break,
He Will Slowly Wave Good-Bye.

Mother of Potions

Cure Us Of All Ills,
You, Mother Of Potions.
Gather Your Ingredients;
Set It All In Motion.

Mix Our Essence In,
Stir Your Cauldron Round.
To You Ever And Always,
We're Eternally Bound.

Grateful For Your Service,
A Vile Is The Prize.
Drinking It Down Slowly,
We Shall All Rise.

Changing Forms And Dear,
We Patiently Do Wait.
For Your Magic Potions,
You Darling, Mother Great.

Priestess of Vengeance

Turn Your Pain Into Power
At The Quaking Altar.
Vengeance Tastes Bitter
But Need Never Falter.

In Wrongful Shame
You Taught Me To Doubt.
But My Strength Is Strong
My Magic Will Reroute.

I Did Not Deserve
The Actions Taken.
Yet Over And Over
I Was Forsaken.

But As A Priestess
I Will Flourish.
Will The Aid Of Hekate
I Am Nourished.

Murderess

They Call You Murderess!
Notorious Desperation
In Your Heart Did Sow.
Safety In Melancholia Lasts.
Sins Have Been Greater,
For Betrayal Warped You.
You Held No Mercy
Within The Laws Of Misery.

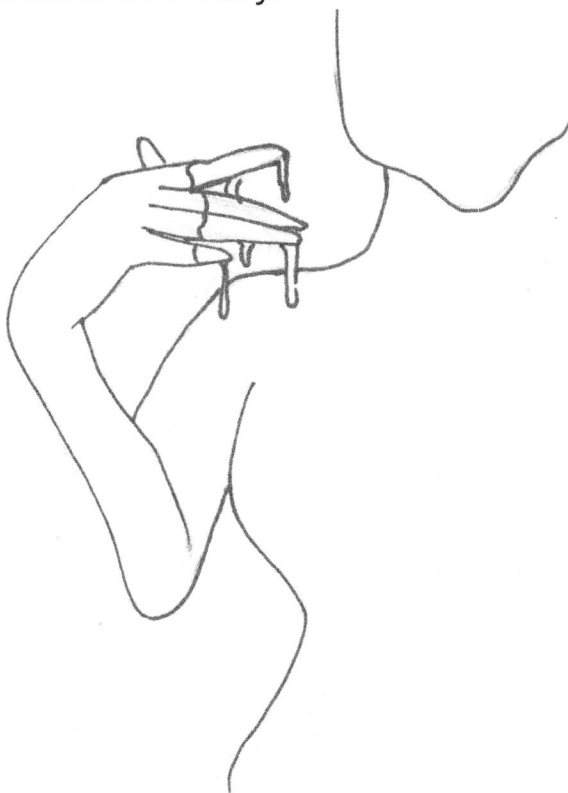

Magician of Trickery

Illusion Is Your Greatest Strength

Setting The Stage For Skeletons.

Play The Piece, Know The Moves.

Drown In Your Beastly Renown,

Ride Through Sneaky Raiders.

Set The Wheel In Motion

Trickery At Its Finest

Magicians All But Linger

In This Noble Humbling Quest

Right The Wrongs Of Kings.

Your Magic Will Take You

Where You Need To Go.

Creature of Cunning

Swirling In An Unending Vortex
You Wield Your Magic
Of Crumbling Cunning Grips.
Abilities Beware The Sacred
Flame That You Harbor.
Necessary Potency Rusts
Cauldrons Bubbling With Insights.
Incant Power Into The
Greatest Realms Of Discourse.
Keen Be Your Breathing Upon
What Needs To Happen.
Lie, Cheat, Steal!
Any Sin Left Standing Goes
Down Into The Spell.
Fool Be Those Lounging
On The Edges Of Your Insanity.

Disgraced Seductress

Disgraced And Betrayed,
You Laughed.
Seducing The Night Cloying
In Your Otherness.
Be It Pride Or Vanity,
Take The Name Of Cursed
Seriously And To Bed.
Making Love To Damnation
And Circumstances
That Failed You.
Simmer Under The Surface,
Made For Coded Messages.
Prisoner To No Thing.
Lurking Along The Edging
Of The Harsh Conditions.
Lounging Next To Betrayal
As Its Controlled Mistress.

Dragon Charmer

Conjure Your Dragons Of The Sun.
Ride The Skies Searching For A Home
That Will Finally Accept You.

Queen Of Notoriety

And In Some Bad Deed
You Were Labeled,
Caught Between Love And Hate.
Monstress In Your Embracing
Cool Blazing Wonders.
Quiet Did You Speak
In The Words Whispered
After Their Clever Names.
Remembering Forgotten Prayers
Rioting Against The Night.
The Fires Were Lit For You.
Banish Shifting Times
Where The Living Knew Existence.
Sovereign Rails Seeking To Play
With Minds Sustained From
The Black Moons Overhead
And Overheard Your
Blasted Notoriety.

TEMPLE OF GOLDEN SORCERY

Cliffed on the Mediterranean Sea, you awaken lying on a sandy dune. Nothing but the wind in your ears. A golden cauldron sits perched on the ledge. Its shine glimmers in the sunlight. Various ingredients surround this glowing vessel. What are they? As you approach, magic fills your being. Lightning sparks from your fingertips. Relevant emotions begin to pile into your mind and heart. You are called to sit by this cauldron and mix up a spell. Which of the ingredients will you choose? When you are seated ross-legged in front of the cauldron, you notice a four-leaf clover just beside you. In the pot it goes. For luck. Now comes the magic!

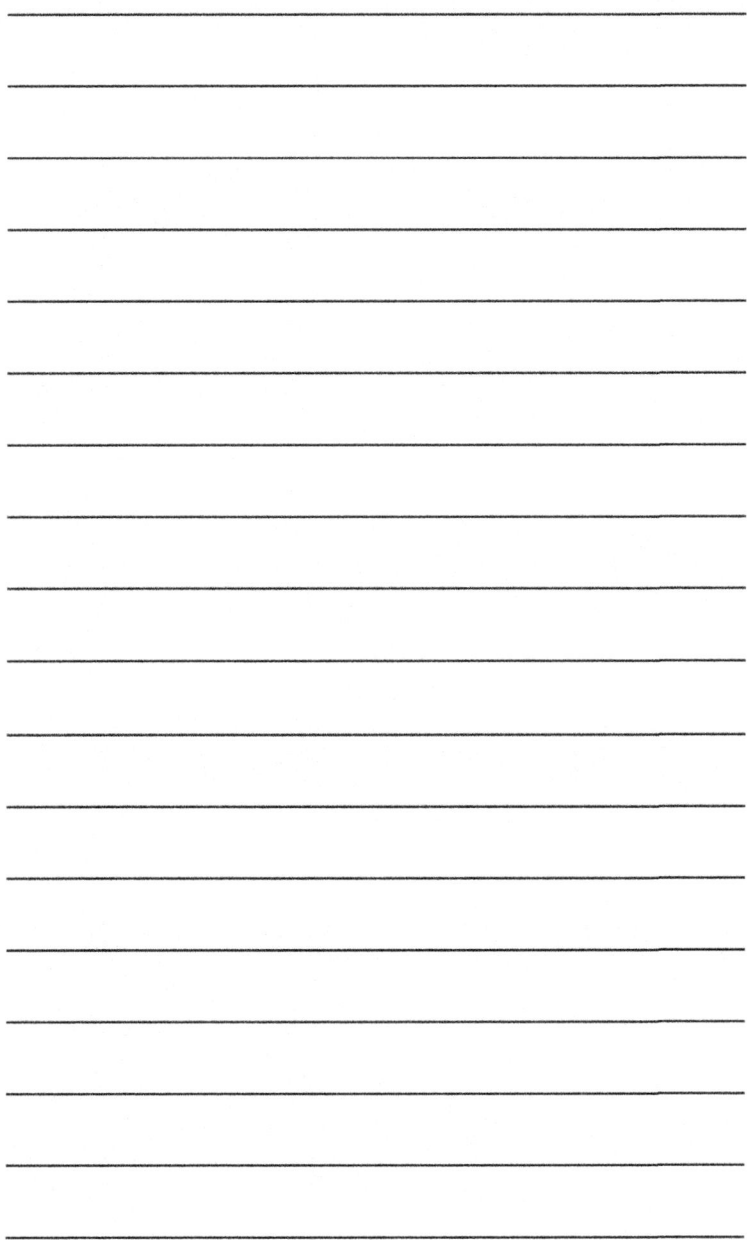

Moirae

Ladies of Cut Cords

Sacrificed On The Altar Of Mortality

The Threads Of Fate Wound Time

Ribbons Left Your Fingers Bloody

Raw From Those You've Cut

Long Or Short Ours Is Yours

Hours Spent With Shears In Hand

Hope Not You'll Cheat Their Slice

Slash Apart The Nights And Days

Rip Aside The Veil Of Tensions

Simulate Sacred Dissociations

Carve Out Varying Circumstance

Sealed Envelopes With Kisses From

The Ladies Of The Cut Cords

Hags of Lawless Lots

Hags Of Lawless Lots
Help Those Who Know Not
The Fates Be Kind
The Fates Be Cruel
Let Decisions Fall
Where They Roll
Guide The Hands
That Want To Know
Which Way
The Path Will Go
Helpless Victims
Of Neutral Truths
Be Ever Vigilant
In Design's Sleuth

Intermediators

Through Legends And Keys
You Know
The Intermediaries Do Flow

In Maps Of All Lines
X The Spot
They Read The Signs

Atlas Of Times Thriving And Still
Marking Deaths
Using Fate's Vulture Quills

Graph Profane Timeline's Plats
Seal Notes
With Them Cannot Combat

Inevitable Maidens

Sundials Spin In Late Shade
Sympathies For No Morrows
Guarding Against Fate Sorrows—
Shatter The Shards Of Destiny
Breaking Apart Waves
Clean And Precise—
No Rotting Chaos Dwells
In The Wells Of Vast Vessels
Perform The Ultimate
Tragedy Of Life Living Entropy—
Comedies Saved Form Lines
In The Corners Of Our Visions
Forget Time Needs You
Play The Role Of Human
Guided By Prop Masters
Disguised In Garb Meant
For Poisoning The Immortal Stage
Set Up Board Backdrops
For Ever Loving Breaking Deaths—
Maidens Take Me And Applaud

Daughters of the Loom

Tethered To You
Oh, Daughters Of The Loom
By Timeless Placenta Threads
Soaked In Afterbirths Of Every One
That Came Before Me.

Standing On Shoulders Of Those
Who Needed Me To Make
Peace With Life And Death.

Represent Me In Living Decay
Coiled By The Ankle Awakened
To Shadowed Mirrored Faces
The Many Tethers Function
Species Molded In Knots.

Have Mercy On The Breaths
Stitch The Charms Upon
Looms Of Universal Woods.

Divine Defining

Define Me In Your Wonderous
Open Valor Bringing
Conjure Up Sweet Destinies
So That Life Will Be Worth Living

Impress Me With Luminous String
Cast Upon My Lonely Shadow
Mountainous Dwellings
A Steep Precipice For Me To Follow

Take Me To New Heights
Sisters Ruling In Majority
Plagued By Time
And Your Divine Authority

Enforcers of Ends

Enforce The Tethers
Count All The Ends
Measure The Threads
With Fate You Tend
(x3)

Mothers of Memory

Deep In The Cauldrons Of Time

Memory Complexes Stir The Pot.

Wade Through Black Floors

On The Periphery Of Eyes Wide

Circumstances Bubbling From The Silt

Frothing Upon Your White Shoes.

The Mothers Are Standing Around

Circling You, Becoming The Memories.

Feeding The Vessel Stewing

Shards Of Recollections Propagate.

Cackling In Sarcastic Loves

Sacred Drought Comes In To Rot.

Static Melts The Ever Changing Basin

As It Becomes Another Memory.

Wyrd Sisters

Hell-broth Churn in the Cauldrons
To the Fates' Plot Pints Of All
Charmed Pools of Solvent
Eyes be to Truths
Portents Foretold Dread Chances
Luck Be, Luck Be
Trouble Brews in Divine Webs
In the Maw of Inevitabilities
Dank Legitimacy, Awful Verity
Froth Build and Run Over
The Tales of Story Untold
Fire Burn and Fates Bubble
Live To Life, Life to Live
SHOULD YE ALLOW!

Fate Charmers

Charm The Slithering Fates
Up From Their Dark Bower.
Sing Them A Sweet Song
Meant Only For Last Hours.

Dancing Raising Quests
For All That Will Partake.
Keeping Balance Strewn
Knowing Not What's At Stake.

Guarded With Talismans
That Have No Bearing Here.
Death Waits On No One
Especially Those With Fear.

Rites And Pact Signed
Laughing All For Naught.
Ever Mortals Hopeful
Fate Will Have Never Forgot.

Ordained Mistresses

Ordained Mistresses,
Meet Me At My Fates;
Cover Me In Your Web;
Seal Me In Due Hastes.

(x3)

Fearless Clippers

Lachrymose, I Stand Unready,
At The Gates Waiting For The
Fearless Clippers Of Destiny;
Cathartic At This Manic Precipice.
Suppress Wanton Reveries Of Death
With Every Emotion Wreaking Havoc
On Hearts Not Yet Codling.
Distance From The Keeper
Laughing At My Compliance
Flying The Keys On Branches.
Flawed And Clawed, Lurking
Modestly Eating My Flesh,
Glued Together With Strings
That Were Meant To Be Tied.

They at the Spool

Initiate Of Life
You Have But Conjured Me Forth.
Fundamental To Essences, Beware
The Cold Breath Of Death I Are Born With.
They At The Spool Move With Graces
Unbeknownst To Us Mortals.
Ceaseless Cruciality Mates With Me
In Your Bringing Fair Uniqueness.
Fragile Longings Await Me
In Life's Most Daunting Obstacles.
Know My Strengths Be But
A Weaving Away From Destinations Seek.
Measure Me A Life Worthy Of Vanities
Rendering Me Vast Dying Entropies.
I Weave Alongside The Fates
Measuring Against The Dying Lights.
Plait Healing Outcomes Only For Me
Twist Me Some Kindred Beloveds.
Let Justice Be Swift For Decisions
Pains Left For Me To Blemish.
Hold My Fate High For Me Weeping
At The Hour Of My Death.

Weavers of Wild

In This Cold And Barren Place
I Tread For Lost Time
Stolen From Fate's Harsh Designs.

Wild Waters And Earth Descend
Upon Me With Tearful Eyes
Strings Woven Can't Describe.

Caught Between The Balance
I Weave And Decide
Predestined Elites Subside.

The Unknown Is Present Here
I've Seen It All Before
Hoping There Was More.

Fate Be These Careful Weavers
When Death Asks Me To Go
I Wish Not To Know.

Seamstresses of Destiny

Seamstresses Of Destinies Fair
Guide Me Upon One's Flare
Shield Me From Fate's Glare
Guard Me As I Lay Bared
Wrap Me In Your Snare
(x3)

Awaken on a hard damp concrete floor. You're in a dark room. You are covered in an incredibly threadbare afghan that seems to be unraveling at your feet. You are twisted in it. The threads lead off to the edge of the room. Pick one thread. What color is it?

Stand up and pull it until it is taut. Shake off the rest of the coverlet. Follow the thread until you come to a dark doorway. There's a dark stairwell here! Follow it down, down, down. It is getting colder as you descend, darker. You make it to an underground level. It is bleak here, your senses are all but erased in this dank place. Something lies in the center of the room.

Where does the thread lead?

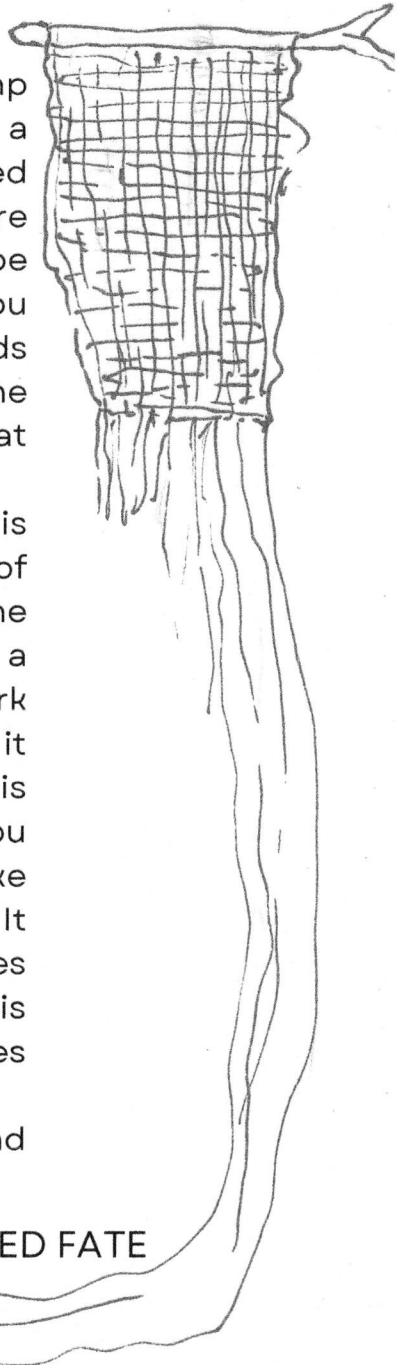

TEMPLE OF TWISTED FATE

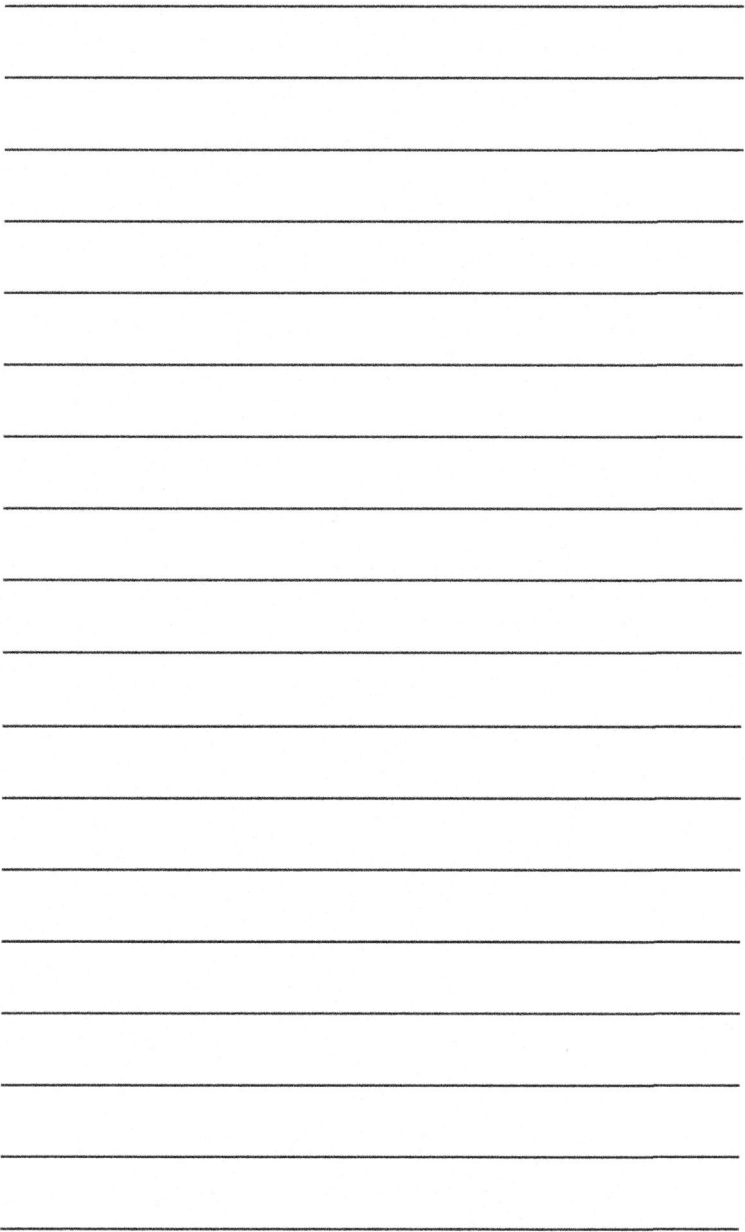

Archetypes

Woman of the Wasteland

Nothing But Wasteland For Miles

Caught The Wind In The Wilds

Gaseous In Wandering Tricks

Grounded In The Apocalypse

Basking In Neon Hued Sludge

Covered In Delicious Grunge

Ravenous Yet Barren

Comforted In Bonfire's Famine

Ruins Useful Places Desolate

Rendering The Mists Derelict

Dancing Wraithlike Wastrel

Never Are You Wasteful

Satisfyingly Trapped In A Daze

Locked Insane In Your Haze

O, Woman Of The Dystopias

O, Woman Of Future Utopias

Researcher of Remarkable

Small Wonders
Found In Paradise's Decree
Holding Precedence In The Hearts
Of All Who Enter The Imagination.
Facts Call Forth Egregious Acquisitions.

Fare Do Your Research,
Critical Minds Hang Webs Of Cognizance.

Investigate The Simple And Complicated.
Examine The Sacred And The Profane.

Studious One Who Turns On Lights
Search The Hidden Realms
Questions May Be Left Unanswered.
All Lay Gigantic Under Your Scrutiny.

You, Who Never Knows Enough.

Nun of Numinousity

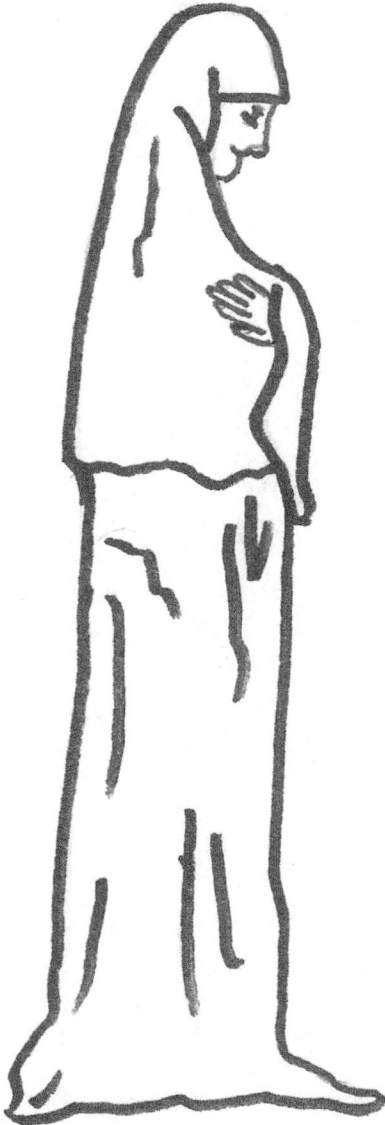

Ascetic Minister Of
Light
Laboring Under
Careful Might

That Which Calls To
You From Voided
Divinities
Trail The Visions Of
Grace Until You're
Free

Darkness Has No
Power Here In Your
Breast
For You Are Honest
And A True
Contest

Ascetic Nun Of
Numinosity
Working Under
Guidance's
Luminosity

Mad Woman

Desperate~
Chained To Norms
Forged Signatures Rotting
Parlors Void
Sentiments Carry Heavy Loads
Flawed In Mannequin
Dressed~
Locked Away Easy
In Reformation's Strangulation
Shoes Too Tight
Roaming Empty Halls
Talking To No One
Rooted~
Devalued In Society
Roles In Cages
Glittering Eyes With Tears Unshed
Biting Tongues Till They Bleed
Wounded With Inequity
Mad~

Huntress Of The Cave

Huntress Emerging
Shallow Cave Situated
Dark Wood Dwelling
Out In The Coming Night
Bat Skat In Her Hair
Moon As A Guide
Target Is Acquired
Sling Back Bow String
Let The Arrow Fly
Predator And Prey
Justice Be Here
In The Shadows
Pick Clean The Bones
Left From Victory
Drag The Carcass
Back, Back
Shallow Cave Situated
Huntress Disappearing
In The Coming Dawn

Wild Woman

Wild Woman, Wild One.
Looking To The Moon And Sun

Hardly Any Worries
Dancing On Your Wild Journey

Nothing You Will Not Confront
Feral In Your Delicate Thrusts

Unfurling Like Petals, Aging Like Wine
Nature Is Your Shrine

Perfumed By The Four Seasons
Adaptive To Any Region

Chasing Rainbows Across The Sky
Iridescent Wings Need Not Apply

Relinquishing Control, Taking It Back
Giving Conformity A Swift Whack

Whirling Inside Even When Still
Inside Boundaries Which You Fulfil

Wild Woman, Honest And True
The Spirit Of Your Soul Guides You

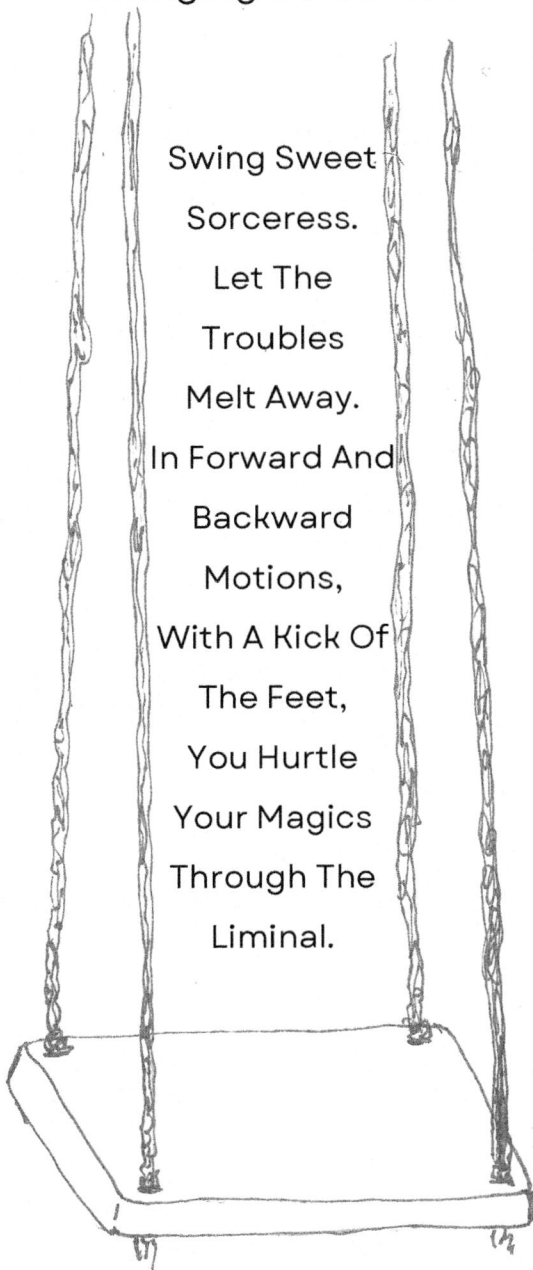

Swinging Sorceress

Swing Sweet
Sorceress.
Let The
Troubles
Melt Away.
In Forward And
Backward
Motions,
With A Kick Of
The Feet,
You Hurtle
Your Magics
Through The
Liminal.

Seeker of Silence

Seek Silence In Quiet Places
Handling The Discourse Of Whirs
Stalking Reticence Down Enchanting Halls
Filled With Thoughts Known Only To You
Swimming In Dreams Of Other Worlds
Drifting Upon Clouds High Above Midnights
Splendor Casts Creature Shadows
Wandering The Forest Of The Mind
Hike To Snow-Capped Peaks
Laughing At Candle Flames Dancing
Breezes Set Out From Your Breaths
Fly Up To Moon From Galaxies Far Away
Unburdened From Gravity's Truth

This Is What Can Happen When You
Seek Silence In Quiet Places

Healer of the Horde

Healer In The Woods,
We Search For Your Wisdom.
Heal Us With Your Many Potions.
May We Choose
From The Corked Bottles?
Nothing But Our Darkest Secret
As Fair Payment.
Which Way To Turn?
What Questions To Ask?
Tasks To Be Mastered?
Right Way Round Back,
Towards The Edge Of Trees,
And Night Descends
Around Our Necks Like Nooses.
Help Us, Help Us.
Healer Of The Horde.

Erotic Enchantress

Sculpt Lust Borrowed
From Honeyed
Tumbles In Orgasmic
Lofts.
Hold Fast The
Melodious Tones Of
The States Of Ecstasy.

Whisper Your Spells In
My Ears.
Cast Your
Enchantment Ridden
On Savior's Distress.

Unzip Weathered
Promises.
Lounge Upon Satin
Charms.
Bearing Nothing But
Luck And Lust.

Unfettered Fae

Escape Beneath The Hills

Following The Golden Light Of Morning

Riding On Rainbow Currents

Telling Stories On The Winds

Bursting Laughter Echoes

Never To Be Lost

In The Forgotten Places

Of This And Other Worlds

Drummer of the Battlefields

Da-Dum Da-Dum Da-Dum

Steady Beat Prologue

Rhythm For Following Ahead

Marching Toward Victory

Marching Toward Righteousness

Da-Dum Da-Dum Da-Dum

Sticks On Drum As You Roam

Excitement Prickles Along The Skin

Dread Threatens To Overtake

A Horn Blows In The Distance

Da-Dum Da-Dum Da-Dum

Crest A Hill At Sunrise

Red Sky Awaits The Party

Ready For Station Formations

Replace Drum For Sword

Da-Dum Da-Dum Da-Dum

CHARGE!

Ecstatic Shapeshifter

Mutate, Agitate
Dance, Twirl, Spin.
Shift Your Shape
In Ecstatic Skins.
Rebuild, Renew
Move, Bend, Turn
Awaken The Senses
In Changing You Learn.
(x3)

Lady of the Labyrinth

Lady Of The Labyrinth,
Longing On The Threshold Of Tall Hedges.
Bursting With Possibilities,
Missed Turns And Dead Ends.

Tying Off Your Dress,
Entranced By Archway Entrance.
You Venture In,
Unraveling As You Attend.

Movement By Instinct.
Laying Out Tiny Breadcrumbs.
Clues For The Journey,
Inward The Monster Tends.

Following Distant Roars.
Senses Alive In Quiet Darkness.
The Lair Is Looming.
Center It Will Defend.

Fight To The Death.
It Needs Your Radiant Inner Light.
Conquering Horned Shadows.
Lady That Transcends.

Princess of Darkness

Through Onyx Halls You Roam
Daydreaming About Witchcraft.

Donned In Black Lace
Glitter On Whimsical Cheeks.
Tempers To Conjure Satan's Wrath.
Immoral Darkness Envelopes You.
Shrouding Mists Float Beneath Your Steps.
Fires Of A Million Stars In Your Bosom.
Abysmal Depths From Kohl-Rimmed Eyes.
Crimson Roses At Your Pale Lips.

Come Forth My Loving Darling.
For You Are The Princess Of Darkness

Captain of Coagulates

Oh, Captain!
You With Ointments
For All Ailments.
Watch Over Festering Skins.
Wounds Inflicted
Inflamed, Raw, Red.
Test Blood's Viscosity.
Caregiver Of Our Scars
Shiny and Purple.
Leech Out The Poison
Pus, Grit, Infected.
Dress In Clean Rags
Tied Off With Teeth.
Thank You Captain
You With Ointments
For All Ailments.
Restored, Anew, Fixed.

Matron of Masks

In This Den Of Anonymity
I Find You.
Luring With Hazel Eyes
Paralyzing In Their Covered Stare.

Have Not You Learned My Name?
Terrorizing To Keep The Charade.
Hiding In Plain Sight
Among The Merry Revelers.

Why The Night Drags
Dripping Like Candle's Wax.
Opulent In Your Touches
On Arms Hot From Dancing.

Matron Of The Masquerade.

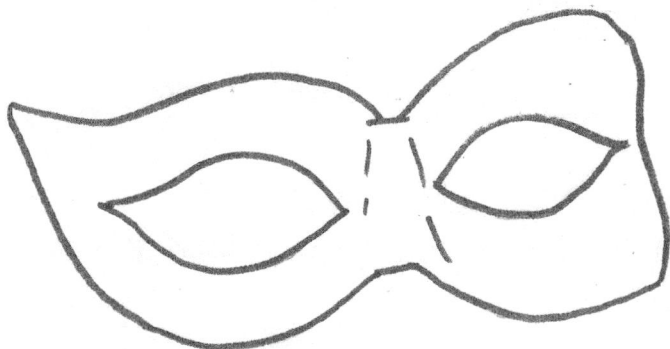

Bone Woman

Hidden In The Soul, Buried All Alone
Collect The Swag, In Deserts Strown

Sift The Mountains, Comb Longings Lost
Find The Bones, At All Costs

Assemble The Wolf, Swirl The Dust
Heart Beneath Ribs, Full-Bellied And Trussed

Sing Over Bones, Still And Sedate
Words Untroubled, Deciphering The Fates

Drum Beat Steady, Shaking Sandy Shores
With Roaring Cackle, Pounce From The Core

Magic In Marrow, Fangs In Shadowed Maw
Flight From Fire, Landing On Paws

Creature Transformed, Laughing As She Runs
Wild Woman Awaken, Never To Be Shunned

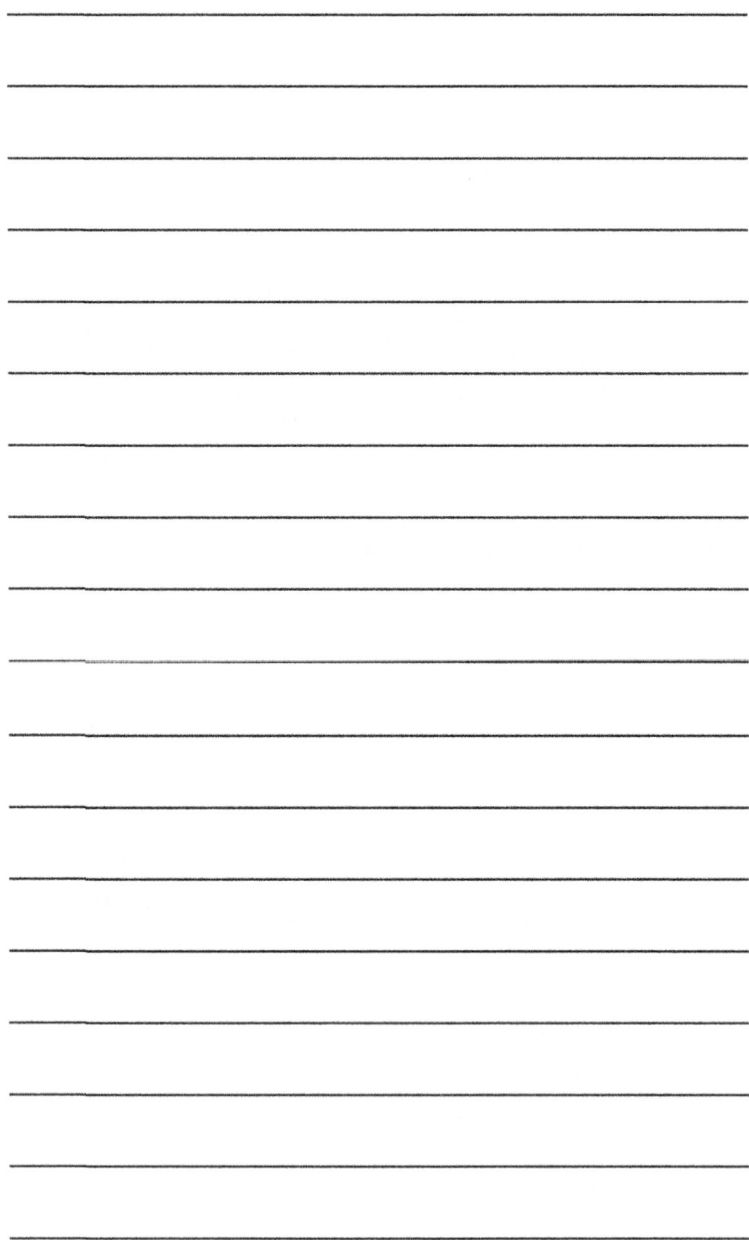

About the Author

Lennan Smith is a poet and artist unlocking doors. She is a seeker and an eternal student of the mysteries of life.
Dancing in liminal spaces and harmonizing her connection to mind, body, spirit, Lennan is impassioned.   She takes an intuitive, visionary approach to her endeavors and thrives on her relationship to imagination.
As a believer and practitioner of magic, she loves to inspire others to find their own place on the web of life.

Find <u>Lennan Smith</u> on YouTube where she shares her thoughts on her many interests.

For More On My Work With

Archetypes

CHECK OUT MY

SYNTHESIS SERIES

"Synthesis Oracle"

"Oracular Synthesis"

BOOK 3 COMES OUT

DECEMBER 2024

Available On Amazon

THANK YOU FOR THE SUPPORT.

Printed in Great Britain
by Amazon